THE PARABOLA
BOOK OF HEALING

THE PARABOLA
BOOK OF HEALING

WITH AN INTRODUCTION BY
LAWRENCE E. SULLIVAN

A Parabola Book
CONTINUUM • NEW YORK

1994

The Continuum Publishing Company
370 Lexington Avenue
New York, NY 10017

Library of Congress Cataloging-in-Publication Data

The Parabola book of healing / with an introduction by Lawrence E. Sullivan.
     p.   cm.
Expanded edition of the "Healing" issue of Parabola magazine (Spring 1993).
Includes bibliographical references and index.
ISBN 0-8264-0633-5 (acid-free paper)
  1. Healing—Religious aspects. 2. Medicine—Religious aspects.
I. Parabola (New York, N.Y.)
BL65.M4P37 1994
234' . 13—dc20

                                                          93-38377
                                                          CIP

The whole question, the only one to which our response is necessary, is whether the circles of our movement tend to become smaller or larger; whether they are closing down to a dwindling point, or opening to a greater and greater inclusiveness; whether or not, in other words, we are journeying toward wholeness. It is all a process, a journey toward; it can never be an arrival. Even our "wholeness" is relative—the measure of our capacity to measure the immeasurable.

—D.M. DOOLING, Focus for the "Wholeness" issue of PARABOLA

When a man finds that it is his destiny to suffer, he will have to accept his suffering as his task; his single and unique task. He will have to acknowledge the fact that even in suffering he is unique and alone in the universe. No one can relieve him of his suffering or suffer in his place. His unique opportunity lies in the way in which he bears his burden.

— VIKTOR FRANKL, *Man's Search for Meaning*

The symptoms of illness become symbols of the state of your being. You are ill but you are not just suffering passively, you begin to see this particular illness as a call to enter into association with powers that are less familiar and to assume new responsibilities.... The goal of many healing rituals is to help the sufferer experience wholeness, which can be experienced through recreating sounds which are whole tones, or through "soundness" of body. The healers chant songs or conduct hubbub, babble, or racket that becomes the emblem of acoustical wholeness. Through the music of the healing rituals we have a suggestion or a glimpse of what that wholeness of sound is about.

—LAWRENCE E. SULLIVAN, Interview, "Healing" issue of PARABOLA

Table of Contents

Healing, Books, and Fascination

Opening this *Book of Healing*, the thought arises: how many books of healing have humans turned to over the millennia? And what is so endlessly fascinating about them that we produce and read them still?

The fascination runs deep. Even the great religious texts that are fountainheads of the scriptured traditions, such as the Bible, the Koran, and the Heart Sutra, are revered by devotees as books of both salvation and healing. For instance, the Ontake-san religious group of Aichi-ken, Japan performs the Heart Sutra and its accompanying mantras in a mountain-top shrine just before walking through fire at the time of the lunar New Year. I attended the rite in 1986. Not only do practitioners chant the words to induce good health in the upcoming year, but they also flash the scripture before their eyes over and over again, unfolding miniature copies of the text rapidly and repeatedly in order to multiply the numbers of "readings" and thus increase the power of healing.

Some of the earliest written records in human history are concerned with health: fragments of health-charms, medicinal recipes, curses that sicken enemies, and prayer-offerings to petition the gods

ix

for recovery from sickness. Decades ago, Walter Jayne, a professor of abdominal surgery at Johns Hopkins, amassed ancient ideas of cure in his book *The Healing Gods*. Jayne argued that this knowledge should be a part of physicans' training because the aim of the medical doctor was to mobilize the patient's "Recuperative Powers," which were only partly biological.

That our fascination with healing is compelling should come as no surprise. We must understand the swings from sickness to health and back because these transitions make us who we are. Sickness is part of each individual biography; every family and social group faces disease. Human life and self-understanding are directed by symptoms, like so many blazes on our path.

We study these pointers during transitions provoked by sickness (or sometimes in the sicknesses provoked by stressful transitions) to know who we are and where we are going. Identity and destiny, being the main marks on the human compass, are sited on forces that flare and reveal themselves in sickness and cure. Caregivers and those concerned with our welfare peer at our bodily signs for messages about the fermenting powers that sickness kneads into our biological and spiritual lives. Whether these messages arrive in the idiom of germs, genes, or *jinns* (embryo-like pathogens that lurk in darkness, according to Islamic medicinal folklore), we set our new course accordingly. What continent is not dotted with holy places and shrines noted for their miraculous cures and the healing power of their relics or amulets? For as long as we have archaeological records, pilgrims have combined their enthusiasm for social gatherings, their interest in tourism, and their yen for long-distance trade with visits to powerful sites of cure, the landmarks of identity and destiny. From the small *jinja* shrines of Japan to the miraculous waters around Tenochtitlan in ancient Mexico, from the Ganges to Lourdes and Rome, signs of healing have focused identities and shaped destinies on the scale of the individual, the community, the empire, and the cosmos.

Sickness and cure are significant moments in the "biography" of religious traditions (and, perhaps, of intellectual movements as well, if we judge by the biographies of such luminaries as Max Weber and Sigmund Freud). Prophets, founders, boddhisattvas, priests, saints, sages, and the gods themselves have dealt with bouts of illness and suffering that are *marked* in the narratives of their traditions. Because the signs of sickness and cure of these extraordinary religious figures prove to be *re-markable*—able to mark the suffering and health of others with a powerful significance—the isolating experiences of many separate individuals can meld, ironically, into broader social traditions based on "shared" experience and mutual understanding. The remarkable signs give rise to religious imagery, symbolic action, common interpretation, and social polity. Recalling these remarkable sufferings and cures in effective ways (through meditation or ritual) can be salvific and salutary.

To read this book with profit, there may be no need for such grand ambitions. Still, one wonders whether reading this book, which contains simply stated but remarkable reflections on sickness and healing, will give rise to shared questions and reflections among its readers— questions about our common destiny, our identity as humans in the cosmos, and the forces that shape us when we respond to them. Bill Moyers began his article in the Spring 1993 issue of PARABOLA with words from the Harvard anthropologist and medical doctor, Arthur Kleinman: "nothing so concentrates experience and clarifies the central conditions of living as serious illness." Will this book, like so many other responses to illness throughout history, create bonds among strangers?

Whether our reader-responses to this book are similar or not, it is certain that questions of sickness and health have played a key role in constituting human history: both in its constructive phases of building up systems and edifices (conceptual as well as physical), which respond to the need for well-being; and in its destructive phases of dismantling irrelevant constructs, when answers pale before more urgent, overshadowing questions.

It seems truly mysterious that the powers of sickness and cure, which traffic so intimately with each human life, remain, finally, hidden and obscure. The irrepressible desire to bring those powers to light accounts for the restlessness of human inquiry, wandering in search of surer knowledge, clearer signs—whether medical or mystical.

That same restless desire explains why so many religious traditions have found sickness and healing—and the impulse to care—to be the paradigm of the human condition in the world.

—Lawrence E. Sullivan,
November 1993

PART I

Metaphors of
Health and Healing

The Remedies

Joseph Bruchac

Half on the Earth, half in the heart,
the remedies for all the things
which grieve us wait for those who know
the words to use to find them.

Penobscot people used to make
a medicine for cancer from Mayapple
and South American people knew
the quinine cure for malaria
a thousand years ago.

But it is not just in the roots,
the stems, the leaves,
the thousand flowers
that healing lies.
Half of it lives within the words
the healer speaks.

And when the final time has come
for one to leave this Earth
there are no cures,
for Death is only
part of Life, not a disease.

Half on the Earth, half in the heart,
the remedies for all our pains
wait for the songs of healing.

Poetry in Buchenwald

JACQUES LUSSEYRAN

Translated by Noelle Oxenhandler

"Hey, Lusseyran! Wait up! Listen!"

The hand of Saint-Jean, thin as a knife-blade, so eager that the bones vibrated like nerves, grabbed my arm. His voice became lower, graver, both angry and tender. He recited,

I know all sorts of people
Who are not equal to their lives
Their hearts are poorly smothered fires
Their hearts
open and close like their doors.

The hand on my arm relaxed, let go, and began gesturing in the air to an invisible witness.

"It's Apollinaire," said Saint-Jean. "Apollinaire! He knew! I tell you, he knew!"

Already my wonderful friend had taken a step away from me. He stood up, lifted his arms. He seemed to have grown taller and to have learned something so essential and so urgent that he had to let me know about it immediately. Yes! It was as though he came bearing news—good news which was going to brighten our wretched lives. I listened to him intently.

I know all sorts of people
Who are not equal to their lives
Their hearts are poorly smothered fires
Their hearts
open and close like their doors.

He recited the verse again, but with a stronger, more confident voice. This time it wasn't necessary for him to convince me of anything. It had become obvious for me as well.

Now he leaned against my shoulder, as if to make me turn about inside myself and examine the horizon with the new eyes he had just given me.

"Apollinaire wasn't thinking about us," he said. "He was thinking about a prostitute, Marizibill. And yet, Lusseyran—!"

There was no need for him to say more. I let him know I had understood. Or rather—I *saw*. I saw around us the ring of sharp rocks that closed off the road, and these men, this multitude of men who were almost faceless and whose eyes open and shut without ever *really* opening. I saw the lines of prisoners who trudged toward the central square to report for work. I saw the cold, the hunger, the fear, all these things that we were not equal to—that were greater than us, too great for us. I knew that the first man I would bump into would not speak my language and would have none of my thoughts. And that for him I, in turn, would be an utter stranger.

As for Saint-Jean, this man who ordinarily asked so many questions, who was so determined to see, to know, to arrive at a simple certainty, a final truth which could sustain him—he gave no further explanations, he sought no further.

I asked, "How did you find these verses?"

"They were there," he said. "I have known them a long time. But it was just then, when I saw the big Russian, a Tartar, and those fifty

6

other Russians who slowly made a circle around him and drew closer in silence and then, finally, threw themselves upon him with cries of hatred and scratched him, trampled him, killed him while nobody did anything or said anything and maybe didn't even *see* anything.... Then, Lusseyran, I understood."

I know all sorts of people
Who are not equal to their lives...

At this my friend made a great gesture with his arm as if to leave unspoken an unbearable thought. This thought had occurred to me in the same instant, and I, too, had found it unbearable. There was this powerlessness of men, our powerlessness, in the face of the events of men's lives, our lives! This was as frightening as the threat of perishing by fire. Bur Apollinaire had *spoken* this powerlessness. He had known how to say it in such a way that it no longer had the same face. It wasn't any softer, but it was clearer. It began to be reclaimed a little bit, just enough to leave a little room in which to live.

I had loved Saint-Jean for several weeks because he was courageous, ardent, agitated, and especially because he had an unbelievable passion which I had never before encountered to such a degree in anyone—a passion for honesty. He didn't ask himself whether or not it was prudent to be honest in a concentration camp. An honest man is honest in all circumstances. One keeps one's word, one tries to understand, even if it's painful. Inner harmony, moral clarity, these are not things to be sold, even at the price of material security—especially not for that.

I had loved Saint-Jean for weeks, this thin, imperious, and driven man, because he *gave* his human voice, his human resonance, with constancy, from moment to moment, in spite of fatigue, the greatest fatigue. I had loved him from the moment I had entered a detention cell at Fresnes, the evening before the departure to Germany. Then I did not know this man who was speaking in the room of sealed windows. But I had been drawn towards him immediately, and without the slightest impulse to withdraw.

He was not a poet. He was a businessman. For many years he had managed a company in Marseilles very successfully. He had been a member of the Resistance from the very beginning in 1940, and a very effective one: he had set up a repatriation network for Allied aviators. He was not a confused daydreamer. And it was he who had suddenly recited Apollinaire, who had suddenly transformed poetry into action.

Some weeks later—this was in the middle of August—during the time that, unbeknownst to us, the Allied armies were liberating France—I found myself in the same spot. I sat on the little stone wall which faced this long and narrow structure: the basins. A door, several high windows, and, in the interior darkness, a line of big red basins, over which hung a sort of metal mushroom from which icy water hissed. Each morning, the moment the night floodlights went out from the tops of the watchtowers, we were herded here and had to clean ourselves in the dense and sweaty atmosphere packed with bodies.

I was sitting on the wall in the sun, between a young Parisian actor—a frightened and too-beautiful young man with the hands of a woman—and a conscientious and somewhat skeptical teacher from Bourgogne. I said to them,

"Poetry, true poetry, is not 'literature.'"

They both cried out,

"Not literature!"

I had surprised, even shocked them. I saw that I would have to explain myself, although I didn't want to. And I began to recite verses, at random, any that I could think of, any that resembled our life at the moment. In a plain, undramatic voice I recited Baudelaire, Rimbaud.

Little by little, another voice was added to my own. I did not know where it came from—I hardly asked myself. Finally, though, I had to listen: the verses were being repeated in the darkness. Voices had timidly joined in behind me, and in front of me. I was surrounded. Without even intending to, I began to recite more slowly.

More men came. They formed a circle. They echoed the words. At the end of each stanza, in each pause, there rose a great hum of the last syllables.

"Keep going! Keep going!" whispered the actor with the hands of a woman, "what's happening is truly extraordinary."

I chanted. It seemed to me in that moment that I knew all the poems I had read, even those that I thought I'd forgotten. The circle of men pressed in closer around me: it was a crowd of men. I heard men who weren't French. The echo which they sent back to me was sometimes disfigured—like the sound of a violin with a loose string—sometimes harmonious. The breath of all these men came closer, I felt it now on my face. There were perhaps fifty of them.

I said to them, "Who are you?" The response came immediately, but in a frightening disorder: some spoke German, others Russian, others Hungarian. Others simply repeated the last words of the last verse in French. They leaned toward me, gesturing, swaying, beating their chests, lisping, muttering, crying out, seized by a sudden passion. I was dumbstruck, happy like a child. The noise had grown so loud in a few seconds that I could no longer distinguish a single word. Far from me, behind the oscillating mob, men hailed the passers-by in all the languages of Eastern Europe. No longer trying to understand what was happening, incapable of feeling anything but happiness, a happiness of the throat and breath, I began to recite again. All I had left in my memory was a poem of Baudelaire: "Death of the Lovers." I recited it. And scores of voices, gravelly, croaking, caressing voices repeated, "The dead flames...."

I had a hard time leaving this crowd, escaping from it. I had to throw my arms out and leave, step by step, still reciting. I know that this is hard to believe, but behind me I heard men weeping.

My teacher-friend told me that all these men wore on their shirts the letter "U": Ungar—they were Hungarians.

"But what happened?" I asked.

"We didn't see anything," my two friends said. "They came from all directions all at once, like flies," said the actor with the hands of a girl. But he who usually snickered at the end of each sentence was now serious and sincere.

In the following days I got to know some of these Hungarians. I learned that most of them were Jews who were waiting for what the S.S. called "transfer to the sky." They all knew they would soon die. I also knew that none of them spoke French, not even a little, but that listening to a man recite poetry, they had thrown themselves upon it as upon food. After a month one of them, Alexander, could repeat without fault the last stanza of "Death of the Lovers"; he could put together all these words which had no sense for him. I asked him what his work was: he was a journalist at Miskolcz, a little village northeast of Budapest.

No, poetry was not simply "literature." It did not belong to the world of books. It was not made just for those who read. The proof of this was growing.

One dark winter morning, in the ink of dawn, we were about thirty exhausted men, shivering, and we were bumping up against each other around one of the red basins for a little icy water. This brutal water, intercepted by a hand, crazed by a face that pressed itself too close, snaked down our naked chests. There was silence, the obligatory silence of all communal activities. But all of a sudden a neighbor began to sing. His voice took off before him and extended out toward us in an immediately magical way. It was the voice of Boris, a man so extraordinary that I can't speak about him just yet. A voice as supple as a head of hair, as rich as the feathers of a bird, the cry of a bird, a natural song, a voice of promise. Without giving notice, Boris had suddenly left this place of cold, dreary dawn and the crowd of human bodies. He recited from Peguy's "The Tapestry of Notre Dame," I think.

Which of us knew what Boris was saying? Who cared? But the thirty of us stayed with our arms held out, leaning forward, a handful of water slipping through our fingers. At last, when the poem was over, a little man whom I had thought for many months was awkward and dull said to me,

"Touch my forehead. It's sweat! That's what warms us up, poetry!"

In fact, the iciness had disappeared. We no longer felt our exhaustion.

❋

One September night, as it was impossible to sleep in the hot and stinking barracks, Sylvain and I stole out and went to the one refuge: the basins. There, there was a little air. Sylvain was a young boy so pale and tormented that he seemed to cry out with each step he took. He had lost all hope, no doubt because being so young, he had not had time before coming to build up enough of a reserve of strength. He watched himself dying, very slowly, gently. He was as patient as he was sad. The hand which he gave me, so stiff that it could only open halfway, I could not touch without the greatest caution.

Sylvain was a little Belgian musician. He had been an excellent viola player, and he had been expected to become a virtuoso. But he didn't speak. Of Flemish origin, French by education, he had never really spoken either language. This night I held his arm very firmly, because he was on the verge of collapse. I wanted to tell him about life, this great subject about which he knew so little. As he didn't understand French well, I recited some verses to him. Little by little, as the hours went by, I felt him grow stronger, his closed hands opened. I heard him begin to breathe. Sylvain was no longer afraid.

Poetry is more than simply "literature."

❋

There was one thing that terror could achieve: that hundreds of men seething in the barracks were silent. Only terror and...poetry. If someone recited a poem, all hushed one by one, as coals go out. One hand drew these men together. One cloak of humanness covered them.

I learned that poetry is an act, an incantation, a kiss of peace, a medicine. I learned that poetry is one of the rare, very rare things in the world which can prevail over cold and hatred. No one had taught me this.

A medicine, neither more nor less. An element which, communicated to the human organism, modified the vital circulation, making

11

it slower, or more rapid. It was, in short, something whose effects were as concrete as those of a chemical substance, I was convinced of this.

A student of books, I had loved poetry as I would have loved a phantom: for its unreality! I had thought that it was simply an "art," a great game, a luxury, and always a privilege. What a revelation!

✻

However, not all the poets were found worthy. Some were not allowed in; they were not welcomed by us in our misery. These were invariably the plaintive and lamenting poets.

Lamartine was not taken seriously: he wept too easily, he pitied himself—something we could not take. Vigny took pleasure in complicating life and was too solemn. Musset—he reached us, in spite of his terrifying egoism, because at least he had the art of song. He was an accomplished actor, a magnificent ham.

Hugo triumphed. The least of his verses gave us a charge, a surge of blood. This devil of a man, this irresistible liver of life entered our lives and mingled with us the moment a word of his was spoken.

He could speak of Charles V, the attributes of divinity, an arm around a pretty waist—he always worked on us. There was no need to understand him, even to listen precisely, to listen to the words: it was enough just to let it happen. Life, in his verses, made the chest swell, caught fire, raced forward. It was also a draught of cool wine in our throats—for drunkenness, the benevolent drunkenness which fills up the empty spots, gives one a new life in place of poverty and pain. We loved Victor Hugo; it was a grand encounter.

Baudelaire also worked on us. But his was a mysterious and cunning power: he had the gift, so rare after all, of finding at the bottom of the darkest holes a little glimmer of light and making it burst before out eyes. He gave meaning to the difficulties of our collapsing bodies. He tied earth back to heaven, linked the real and the impossible—with a flourish that gave us courage. It was permitted, then! Then we, too, were going to do it. In the stolen cigarette, in the crummy pipeful of dried grass, we were going to breathe all the lost paradises. He did it so well.

But the real winners, the tonics, those who worked upon us like a wine, were the poets who sang. I found some in the Middle Ages. Then there were Villon, Ronsard, Verlaine, Apollinaire, Aragon. They surmounted all obstacles. They spoke from another realm. Or rather, it was their step, the rhythm of their gait, which had nothing in common with our cowering. They flew past and carried us on their wings.

Can I remember that this is not just a manner of speaking, that for us these were sensations, that poetry was completely lived by us, and not simply evaluated? We didn't say, "It's beautiful," an expression which only has meaning for those who are happy, the sated. We said, "You see how much good it does!"

I hear skeptics growling, "He's not going to tell us that they were *fed* by poetry." Of course not. We were nourished by a watery soup and a bitter bread. And by hope. Let skeptics not forget this! It was precisely in this matter of hope that poetry acted upon us. And it was in the thick of these most completely physical, material circumstances which I endured even to the point of suffocation, that I understood how utterly tangible are these things without weight which we call hope, poetry, life.

The little worker from Lens whom I consoled, whom I nourished with the only thing that remained to me on that day, a poem of Eluard, never pushed away this morsel which I held out to him. He never called it "play money." For him it had the most real existence: it was a chance to run, a rope to grab onto. It had a weight in the throat which reached, with one great thrust, towards the future.

To nourish the desire to live, to make it burn: only this counted. Because it was this that deportation threatened with death. It was essential to keep reminding oneself that it is always the soul which dies first—even if its departure goes unnoticed—and it always carries the body along with it. It was the soul which first had to be nourished.

Morality was powerless. All moralities. As if they had been created by artificial conditions of existence: provisional peace, provisional social equilibrium. Ideas, knowledge, could do nothing either: they left despair intact.

Only religion nourished. And next to it, the sensation of human warmth, the physical presence of other human beings. And poetry.

Poetry chased men out of their ordinary refuges, which are places full of dangers. These bad refuges were memories of the time of freedom, personal histories. Poetry made a new place, a clearing.

I met a modest and gentle man. His name was Maurice. I rested near him, because there was no violence in him, not even hidden. Each day he had the same serene expression; he spoke in short, abbreviated sentences. He looked at life from far away, always from very far away. It was as though there was a window between it and himself. Maurice was very sentimental. He was afraid of imposing himself on others. So normally he didn't speak, or else he simply repeated in a solemn way the last words of each sentence of whoever was talking to him.

Maurice had been an accountant in a firm at Saint-Etienne. He had very few memories, but those he had pained him terribly. They all centered around a woman, his wife. I listened to him intensely because it was the first time in months that a man had spoken to me of his legitimate loves and been overcome by emotion.

Maurice had a wife who was not particularly pretty, as he was always repeating, but who was his, who had always consoled him, supported him, and whom, certainly, he would never forget. His voice tightened when he made this promise, as though his return to this woman was forever impossible.

He spoke of Simone's hands, her hair, her heart, her dreams. He spoke of her personality and of her body without the slightest distinction. For him, all of Simone had the same tender and bitter taste.

He spoke to me about her one time, two times, ten times. At last one day I saw that this man was devouring himself. These memories were killing him. "I shouldn't think of her like this," he said. "It's too real. I know. But what can I do?" And one day I thought of poetry. I drew my accountant into a corner and recited to him a poem from Eluard which Saint-Jean had taught me:

She is there on my eyelids
And her hair is in mine,
She has the form of my hands,
And the color of my eyes,
She is engulfed by my shadow
Like a stone under the sky
Her eyes are always open
And do not let me sleep
Her dreams in broad daylight
Evaporate the suns
And make me laugh, cry, and laugh
And speak without having anything to say.

Maurice listened, said nothing, left. But the next day at wake-up time, he stopped me at the barracks' entrance.

"You know, my friend," he said, "since you told me that poem I haven't been thinking of her in the same way. I see her, but it doesn't hurt anymore. She seems to be everywhere, rather than being at Saint-Etienne. Your Eluard has cured me."

It was true. He spoke so much more loudly, firmly. He was for awhile at least, cured of himself.

※

I threw myself into a poetry campaign.

In the middle of the block, at midday, I stood upon a bench. I stood there and recited poems. I was the neighborhood singer and passers-by stopped. They pressed in around me. Soon other voices answered mine. I felt them all so close to my body that I could hear the in-and-out of their breath, the relaxation of their muscles. For several minutes there was harmony, there was almost happiness.

Unhappiness, I saw then, comes to each of us because we think ourselves at the center of the world, because we have the miserable conviction that we alone suffer to this point of unbearable intensity. Unhappiness is always to feel oneself imprisoned in one's own skin, in one's own brain. For a few moments there was none of this: the poets,

15

the great poets, spoke the universal, spoke of a world in which all beings exchange strength and weakness, youth and decrepitude.

Simone, Maurice's Simone, was forever no longer at Saint-Etienne. These men and myself were no longer at Buchenwald, and there only, forever. How this helped us to live!

✳

Books were rare, as one can imagine. Some came to us rolled up in food wrappers, crushed in the middle by a hunk of wood. Mutilated books circulated.

And it was thus that one morning the Greek text of the first section of *The Iliad* and a German translation came enveloped by thick spongy rolls of synthetic sausage.

I decreed a mobilization of our memories. I made each man recite whatever verses he knew. Bit by bit I put together poems. I discovered that in men's minds there are great springs of poetry and music which nobody in ordinary life thinks of tapping.

Boris—the one who sang Peguy at the basins—said to me one day, "My child, my child" (as he called everyone he loved). "My dear friend! I beg you to count up everything that is not yours. Your hand is yours, your body is yours, your ideas are yours. What poverty! But poetry, it's not yours. Nor mine nor anyone else's And that's why it gives us life. Let's not speak of anything else, O.K.? Only poetry, and love."

It is in part because of this experience that I will say without ceasing, "Man is nourished by the invisible. Man is nourished by that which is beyond the personal. He dies from preferring their opposites."

Images of Wholeness

AN INTERVIEW WITH LAWRENCE E. SULLIVAN

Lawrence E. Sullivan, a student of Mircea Eliade and Associate Editor of The Encyclopedia of Religion *(New York: Macmillan, 1987), has written extensively on questions of the body, health, and healing from the point of view of the religions of the world. He is the editor of a comprehensive survey of these subjects entitled* Healing and Restoring: Health and Medicine in the World's Religious Traditions *(New York: Macmillan, 1989). His book* Icanchu's Drum *(New York: Macmillan, 1989) won Best Book awards from the American Publishers Association and the American Council of Learned Societies. Dr. Sullivan is the Director of the Center for the Study of World Religions at Harvard University. In October, 1992, we spoke to him at his office in Cambridge.*

— Ellen Draper and Virginia Baron

PARABOLA: Since so much of the work you have done centers on healing and on health issues, we would like to begin by asking you to speak about the relationship between health and religion.

LAWRENCE E. SULLIVAN: If we take a cue from the different religious traditions themselves, it seems to me health and healing are a natural subject matter in the study of religion. When you look at the lives of the founders of those traditions, whether it was Zarathustra, Buddha, or Jesus, you find they were exemplary in terms of encouraging health. They had a penchant not only for curing people's ills physically, but also for holding up some notion of health, or wholeness, or well-being, offering people a new vision of their relationships with one another and their relationships with the world around them. So I find healing is a central issue, because it asks meaningful questions about religion itself.

P: You use the terms "curing" and "healing." What is the difference between them?

LES: Cure would be the elimination of the disease or of the state of illness in a community, where healing would focus on the individual who is suffering from sickness and bring him or her back to a state of health.

Although religions can address both dimensions of the question, first and foremost, they are directed to healing this particular individual suffering, this circumstance. This situation can be rendered significant.

P: What is that significance?

LES: The symptoms of illness become symbols of the state of your being. You are ill but you are not just suffering passively, you begin to see this particular illness as a call to enter into association with powers that are less familiar and to assume new responsibilities.

P: You mentioned the relationship between health and wholeness. Ordinarily we look at wholeness as the status quo: somebody is sick, which means that he has come apart and he needs to get put back together again. How do you look at wholeness in the religious sense?

LES: In the mythologies that I'm most familiar with—Central African and South American—wholeness is largely inaccessible or very difficult to access in this world's condition. However, the healing scenario presents to the sufferer images of wholeness, which are primarily images of a time which is no longer available, which can only

18

be described in mythic terms, or can only be enacted symbolically through performances and rituals. To experience wholeness of the body, or wholeness of time, you have to work backwards in time. For example, the Mapuche people use music to overcome infertility. According to Carol Robertson, the Mapuche distinguish everyday song from *tayil*, which is the acoustical overtone of an inherited patrilineal soul. *Tayil* is the only manifestation of this invisible soul, a temporal organ stretching back into mythical time.

The Mapuche perform their *tayil* in a ritual moment called *Entun Kuifi* ("pulling the ancestors"), during which a female musical specialist, the *witakultruntufe* ("she who carries the drum") calls the roll of patrilineal souls in a litany that reaches back in time to the *alüaluntu*, a mythical era that includes all realities more than four generations old.

At sunrise, to the accompaniment of libations, male adults chant their *tayil*, as the sound-time stuff is pulled from their mouths by the *witakultruntufe*. Her strength allows her to draw the separate time-lines from the breath of the chanting men, each from a distant patrilineage, and weave them into a single fused time-line in her mouth.

The *tayil* has four phases, each one corresponding to a space-time world through which the performers must pass as they follow the threads of their patri-songs back to the mythical world of the first ancestors. The *witakultruntufe* is said to "cut" her way through these space-time zones. She forces the air of the patriline chants through her clenched teeth, cutting through time with the knife of her teeth. Her clenched teeth also act as a barrier, keeping the pathogenic evil of this world away from the pure, healing powers of the mythical beginnings of time. The time-transcending lineage songs convey prayers to the supernatural powers of the fullness of time. All the time-lines merge in the din and babel of performance to recreate the wholeness of mythic time in sound.

The goal of many healing rituals is to help the sufferer experience wholeness, which can be experienced through recreating sounds which are whole tones, or through "soundness" of body.

The healers chant songs or conduct hubbub, babble, or racket that becomes the emblem of acoustical wholeness. Through the music of the healing rituals we have a suggestion or a glimpse of what that wholeness of sound is about.

P: The wholeness that you're talking about is in the past, and you're speaking of traditional, indigenous societies. What about Western religion? In terms of Christianity, for instance, it seems to me that wholeness would be in the future.

LES: Yes. Christianity has an eschatological propensity to look toward the end of time as the fulfillment of time. You find this in the Scriptures and in the Gospels, where there is perhaps a residue of Zurvanism or other concepts of time preceding Christianity. Even in contemporary Christian healing practices, notions of the wholeness of time and of sound are fundamental. In Pentecostal Christianity and healing traditions, the image of Babel is reversed: sounds are dispersed, separated. In the Acts of the Apostles (Acts 2:1-47) there are gatherings in the Upper Room and in the Temple of Jerusalem, where all the different winds and sounds are heard as a single language, the gathering up of all breathing cultures into one unison. In contemporary Pentecostal healing scenarios, you have the same hubbub, the in-gathering of the tongues, as a sign of being in the presence of the spirit. Each tradition articulates this working towards wholeness in its own way.

But the healing of Christianity is not inherently future-oriented. Piero Camporesi has shown that the apothecary herbs and medicinal spices which arrived in Europe after the commerce of the Crusades fit into a cosmology of salvation already articulated in folk belief and in the theology of Bonaventure's *Tree of Life*. In this view, healing plants flowered in Eden before the fall, but the life-giving branches never ramified into history, for they were severed when humankind was banished from Paradise. Through the cross, Christ regrafted humanity to the creative tree of life in Paradise. The bodily fluids that flowed from him at the time of his salvific passion and death represent the reflowing of the vital resins and balms of Eden. They gave rise to the medicinal plants, unguents, and aromatics brought from the Holy Land to Europe. Like the incorruptible bodies of saints, which exuded the odor of sanctity, the apothecary was a sign of the healing powers of creation, now flowing through the branches of human history.

P: There is a relationship, it seems, between the concepts of time and sound in the process of healing.

LES: That's right. Speaking in general about sickness in terms of time, you notice the image of wholeness of tone in many of the calendrical rituals which mark the occurrence of time. In New Year's festivals, for example, there is the celebration of din or racket, babble, as a stylized song, in which the whole community participates. A very common feature of New Year's celebrations, whether in the tribal societies of many continents, or in New York City's Times Square, is the notion that you begin again with a whole fresh unit of time, and you can mark that beginning, really call it into existence through sound. The word "calendar" is after all derived from a Greek word, *kaléo*, meaning "to call" or "to summon," a verb centered in the active world of sound. New Year's din is intended to summon or ring in a *healthy* new year, pure and prosperous.

P: You have spoken of healing in terms of the wholeness of time and of sound. How do you see it in terms of space?

LES: In looking at sickness, healing, and restoration, one recognizes that the body is, among other things, a space. For it to suffer sickness is some dislocation of space, some disorientation in space. Part of overcoming illness and restoring health is to regraph the person in his or her own space. The physician must also be a physicist, familiar with all the dimensions of the spatial world. You can see this portrayed in Navajo sand paintings, in which beauty is a recomposed wholeness, relocating the person in colors and relationships drawn from earlier, multiple spatial worlds. You can see this in other healing traditions as well, where a lot of the effort is the reregulating and reordering of space, the reimagining and refashioning the cosmos, but not always in a rote fashion: it is sometimes refashioned very creatively and idiosyncratically around the particular individual who is suffering.

P: In your writings, you mention the term, "the history of the body." Would you say something more about that?

LES: In different cultural and medical and religious traditions the body is a combination of many various elements which may house various spiritual elements or souls, or names, or images, each one of which might have a history of descent. In some groups from the south Central Amazon, for example, the right shinbone represents or houses an element of soul which descends through the father's line; blood has a history of descent through the mother's line. In these cases, the body is a recombinant reality. At each way station of the life cycle, in the rituals of life's passages, these recombinations further rearrange the mosaic, or add new pieces to it, or polish and disclose different facets of the body and where it came from. The history of the body, especially the mythical history, becomes very important; the human body can become a cipher of travel through time. As you grow older and are made aware of different aspects of your body and its functions and the kind of history that attaches to that, you open backwards through time.

Cellular biologists are telling us that we are also combinations of earlier histories, showing us that within each cell there are mitochondria with deposits of DNA which pre-exist the human species. In a strict sense, as Lewis Thomas once put it, the centers of our cells are not ours but the descendents of colonial prokaryocytes that migrated into the ancestors of our eukaryotic cells to settle there. They have DNA and RNA different from ours. Our human bodies are shared, rented, or inhabited by beings with lives and histories of their own. Thinking of it in those terms, the body and its cells represent a history of life forms in the universe that preexist humanity, a history that links all organic, recombinant life in the world.

P: So as the body is progressing through life and as each new chapter of its history is being written, are there certain moments of passage which are dangerous, or where there is more of a risk, in terms of illness? And might the same moments exist, on the level of being?

LES: That's right. Think of key moments of growth, spiritually and physically, as an encounter with other forces in the universe. The optimal recombination of the human personality and the human body—to grow well, to be healthy—requires that the body be at an intersection of spaces and times. Various forces or powers come

22

together there during schooling, adolescence, marriage, parenthood, and in ceremonial rhythms of economic and political life. This intersecting of different forces can go awry. So the call to be mature is at the same time a call to run the risk of disorientation, of illness, and sickness. There's an identity between our religious vocation of living a full symbolic life, encountering other kinds of realities and powers through the symbolic performance of rituals, and the fact that we are ill and suffering, which is the consequence or complement of the challenge to evolve. So we return to the questions about being human, about being religious, about being involved in medical negotiations and restoring people to health: they all seem to be the same process, to involve the same intentions.

P: How do you measure the effectiveness of the healing practices in traditional societies? That's probably a very Western question, but we don't exist in isolation, and there are causes, external causes, for most problems—the introduction of Western diseases to other cultures, for example. When we see some of the traditional healing practices we can be tremendously impressed, and yet not know how well they work.

LES: I think in general this is a problem: how can we really get a fix on the efficacy of different kinds of therapies? To a large extent every healing system is effective or it would not survive; each one has a satisfactory way of explaining how its operations are a success even if patients die. All patients eventually die and any system of treatment must establish its effectiveness in the face of this challenging reality.

Measuring efficacy is an especially acute problem in dealing with traditional societies in Africa, South America, Oceania, and different parts of Asia. It is difficult enough to make sure that adequate health care is being provided, never mind "looking on" at the same time, in order to measure effectiveness in a reliable and controlled fashion in terms that might satisfy biomedical scientists.

One aim of healing practice that is often very effective in local terms is to create an operating "theater," a spectacular setting where the forces of affliction and powers of cure can be put on display in a

23

dramatic way. Cure almost always has a "miraculous" quality: setting on visible display the forces that might otherwise remain hidden and unillumined. Medical practice is effective, then, because it is revelatory, disclosing and naming transformative powers that are active but unrecognized.

P: Whatever interpretation you make, whether from an indigenous, an Eastern, or a Western point of view, this interpretation is still based on a certain worldview, which tells us what wholeness or wellness *is*. In order to judge the efficacy of any given healing practice, we would have first to define what we mean by wholeness, what we mean by wellness.

LES: Yes. And then the question is, what realm of experience or thought or reflection provides an adequate sort of overarching image of wellness? In many of the world religions images of well-being and salvation merge. Such was certainly the case for Zarathustra and Jesus and for the Healing Buddha. And the convergence of ultimate health and salvation does not seem limited to the major world religions, if one may judge by the evidence of millennial movements in Papua New Guinea, or among Maori prophets in New Zealand, or Guarani eschatological leaders in South America. This has been one of the questions raised about biomedicine, particularly in reference to pathology, which gives us better images of what disease might be than what images of wellness might be. This seems to be an issue among the various allied health professions. Nurses provide better images of normal health, of preventive care, and of education than do physicians, whose primary history is that of the study of pathology and disease. And then there is the religious point of view. Religions are primarily concerned with images of health, not only in relating to individual desires and experiences, but also with the larger question of the health of humanity. For that reason there is a desire on the part of sufferers and practitioners to continue to make creative interweavings of images of well-being derived from religion and other spiritual sources on the one hand, and with care, hospitalization, and treatment on the other.

P: There are certain things that happen to all of us—we are born, we get older, and eventually we all die—and our attitudes towards that process are very different. One person's view of wellness is some-how to avoid getting older and dying. In other societies, death is part of the natural order of things: wellness exists within the framework of aging and dying. Could you say more about that?

LES: In fact, it's interesting to see this association of death with old age, which comes so naturally to us in the West today. In some societies this connection is highly unnatural, because only a rare few live to old age. In these societies, death is more often associated with children who die, or mothers who die in childbirth. So, there is a shifting set of natural associations. The notion that all people die and that this is something we must confront as human beings is an issue about the very nature of religion.

P: Could you think of death as one of those moments of passage you spoke of earlier?

LES: Yes. You see death inserting itself, interrupting at these points in the life cycle where there is an intersection of the forces of space and time. Of course, death is a rite of passage in itself. Funeral ceremonies, often elaborate and extended over years of time, aim to bring about the proper ritual end to a life ritually evolved. The funer-al disposes of the spiritual and physical particles of the person in their proper cosmic realm.

Interestingly, death is not limited to its one moment at the end of life. For mortal beings, images of death punctuate most points of growth and change throughout the life cycle. Death symbols pop up in ceremonies of birth, naming, marriage. Victor Turner noticed that Central African societies treated young initiates as corpses in their puberty rites, since they are dead to what they once were but not yet reborn in their new condition.

In Roman Catholic liturgies for the ordination of priests, for example, just before the bishop lays his hands on the ordinand's head, the candidate lies prostrate and motionless in symbolic death while the congregation chants names of the dead over him. Immediately afterwards, he rises to a new life and, through the imposition of the bishop's hands, his soul is imprinted with a new character by the Holy

Spirit. From then on, having experienced a new, ritual death and ris-ing in Christ (as he did in baptism), the priest is able to administer the sacraments of healing the sick, as well as others.

P: What can you say about the view of death as a solitary experi-ence as opposed to being part of a community, or having a guide who helps you? It seems to me that society today has almost lost that sense. There are so many people who die alone; there is the attitude that dying is something you have to do by yourself.

LES: In different societies, so many passages over the gulf of death are made with the help of some guide or sponsor who provides a ritual companionship at these critical moments. This sponsor could be a person of another generation, a partner in commerce, or one's hus-band or wife.

You were speaking earlier about the introduction of disease by one culture to another, and one thinks of how the contact between Europeans and aboriginal people proved to be devastating, in terms of disease. Population historians estimate that the population of native South America was reduced by nine-tenths or more in the first one-hundred-and-twenty years of contact.

I want to point out that at the same time, Europe itself was being swept with diseases which decimated the population in an unbelievable way. In 1507 in Toledo, in Spain, typhus wiped out nearly half of the city's population. There was also smallpox, and the bubonic plague.

P: Could you look at these epidemic diseases as another expres-sion, on a larger scale, of what a human life goes through at moments of danger, by risking death and disease? Could you say that the planet itself somehow goes through these kinds of moments, which are very dangerous?

LES: This is exactly the point I was aiming to make, that the encounter of different peoples was seen in religious terms, certainly among native peoples but also many times on the part of their European counterparts. It was a religious, eschatological scenario which native America had already built into its mythologies: worlds had come and gone several times, some of them on a regular cycle,

26

and some of those cycles came very close to the time of contact. The reading of their religious landscape was that it was a dire time, when the world was coming to an end. In this reading, disease and death on a mass scale played their roles. Native chroniclers, such as Guaman Poma de Ayala of Pern, recognized epidemic disease symptoms as the dominant symbols of their day, signifying the disastrous consequences of the convergence of peoples with diverse histories or morals and distinct supernatural forces present at their origins.

P: Do you see that in all traditions and all religions there is a need to identify the cause, to fix the blame, or take on the guilt related to disease?

LES: The identification of all relevant relationships, both causal and consequential, often comes up in the context of divination, in which nothing is insignificant or random. Divination discerns the causes of the problem through an examination of all of one's relationships and responsibilities.

In the religious sense, one dimension of the way human beings face disease, whether on the scale of individual sickness, or in epidemics on a massive scale, has been to conjure the image of the whole, where the possibility of divination and purification lie.

P: What is the role of artistic creativity in healing?

LES: So much of the creativity of a culture is a response to the possibility and the reality of sickness and disease, whether this be in the realm of oral tradition or written literature, music, dance, visual art, or the festival mobilizations of communities. Healing always points toward a renewal of creative powers, toward a condition that is vital, stirring, strong and whole, as befits a creative beginning. Art embodies and expresses these creative virtues, which link art inextricably to healing. A glance is sufficient to recognize that creativity is spurred on by sickness: the music and dance of the Hamadsha, a medical Sufi brotherhood of Morocco; the role of the cure of the Empress in the acceptance of Buddhism in Japan; the *Spiritual Exercises* of Saint Ignatius, written during his recuperation; the ingenious dietary and hygienic systems, such as Ayurveda and Levitical laws, which classify a world of foods, actions, and relations with systematic precision; the Grail cycles of literature, in which the "sickness" of the Fisher King affected the vitality of the world. In all the major cities of the world today, hospitals and medical research centers, responding directly to sickness, choreograph the creative ideas, research, and resources of thousands.

One reason people are so creative in relation to disease is because it is there that they face elementary forces that both constitute and decompose them. In the symbolism attending sickness, the presence and nature of such forces are revealed. That is why, as I think I mentioned earlier, medicine is always miraculous. It makes visible, for all to see, the powers that otherwise remain invisible outside of the critical context of sickness and suffering.

In many ways disease and episodes of sickness remind people that meaning is an achievement. The notion that human beings live meaningful lives is both a problem and a promise. In the face of disease and other challenges that becloud meaning or disclose it in painful glimpses, you are impelled to try to discover, clarify, or achieve meaning through creative expression.

A Day in Court

THOMAS A. DOOLING

"Thou shalt love the Lord thy God with all thy heart, and with all thy soul, and with all thy mind. This is the first and great commandment. And the second is like unto it. Thou shalt love thy neighbor as thyself. On these two commandments hang all the law and the prophets."   —Matthew 23: 37-40

In these words Christ summed up the central task of this life's spiritual work: We are not only "called" from without to explore and develop this constellation of relationships, but seem moved from within by a longing to do so. Something within us yearns for "rightness," for a lively awareness of being in relationship, not only with the Almighty, but also with our fellow human beings.

Perhaps this dual, harmonious relationship is that state which we call "wholeness." Linguistically, "wholeness," "wellness," and "health" mean the same thing. For many, it also means the Godhead.

We define variously the awful chasm between where we are and where we would be as "sinful," "sick," "ill," and "bad." Like Miss Clavell, the caregiving nun in the old children's story, sometimes we awaken in the middle of the night with the sure and awful knowledge that something is not right. We reach for wholeness, we struggle for it, and most of us, like the little student Madeleine, pray for a Miss Clavell to appear in the night to make us whole, to help us, guide us, teach us, or do *something* to help bridge that terrifying gap of incompleteness. In the language of the Anglican Book of Common Prayer, we sense that we have done that which we ought not to have done, that we have left undone that which we ought to have done, and that there is no health in us.

The very language we use to describe the different aspects of our alienation from completeness speaks of illness on the one hand, reconciliation and healing on the other. Yet so much of the fragmentation that is a substantial part of our individual "illness" has become institutionalized in our social and political structures, as though the different aspects were not connected to each other, all part of the same thing.

Our spiritual, mental, emotional, physical, and "temporal" health are, in fact, linked: they are different aspects of the same wholeness— or its lack. We really shouldn't need to look in different places for that which will heal us, and those whose function it is to make wholeness out of this fragmentation ill-serve that wholeness by compartmentalizing it.

Today we are beginning, tentatively, to realize that at least some "healing" specialists must pay more than lip service to the longing for wholeness of those who ask for help: Psychiatrists recognize the necessity of including the "spiritual element" in treating behavioral disorders, priests recognize that spiritual malaise may produce physical symptoms, and physicians recognize that the material conditions of their patients' lives have a profound effect on their physical health.

It is perhaps a symptom of our problem that we use the peculiarly redundant phrase "holistic medicine" to describe one manifestation of this phenomenon. All healing, medical and otherwise, should be holistic. Perhaps the disfavor of the term "healer" among even those who cope with the most obvious manifestations of illness is a measure of how wide the gap is between our present state and wholeness. Healers now regard themselves as mere technicians who limit their involvement (and their malpractice liability) by treating only one specific symptom, leaving the patient, like Macbeth, in all other ways to "minister to himself."

If the *soi-disant* "healing" professions are narrow, technical, and anti-holistic, surrendering to the very forces of fragmentation and alienation which created the problems they are dedicated to solving, how much worse is it that some healers cannot or will not perceive themselves as healers at all? Lawyers, whose function is to create wholeness, to mend rifts in social relationships, often view themselves instead as "white knights" or even as hired guns.

But, by definition, ought not members of the legal profession be healers? Is not the making of wills, the writing of contracts, the adopting of children, the buying and selling and making of deals, "preventative law?" Is not reconciliation the prevention of alienation? Healing the avoidance of wounding? Do not, or should not, lawyers and the legal system perform these functions?

It is in the nature of healing to be procreative: that which has been healed is greater than the broken parts from which the wholeness was assembled. One who has been "healed," however partially, in a spiritual or medical sense, is often better off than before the illness became acute. Could not this be true for law as well?

The courtrooms of the Western world are littered with broken promises, failed expectations, broken relationships, and living complainants (or dead ones championed by the prosecutors and forces of law and order) complaining, literally, of broken bones, bodies, and lives. Criminal courts understand that for their mental and emotional health the victims or survivors of criminal activity need some involvement in the trial, prosecution, conviction, and punishment of the author of their injury.

In fact, if contracts prevent illness in material relationships, then litigation restores wholeness to those social and material relationships which have been damaged or broken. This recognition could be the key to recognizing that the law and its applications, at their best, serve to reconcile and heal social wounds. Unfortunately, lawyers tend to view the process as one of vengeance or "getting even," not as one of restoration of wholeness or healing.

Anglo-American jurisprudence, as have its European, Roman,

Greek, and Mosaic predecessors, wrestled for centuries with attempts to reconcile the purely human desire to "get even" and the equally human, if somewhat more divinely inspired, desire to make things right. A community wounded by the wrongful act of one of its members needs to satisfy itself that things are whole again, that the breach of human relationships has been resolved. Yet, no matter how contrite a wrongdoer is at the bar of justice, we never really trust his protestations of reform, and in many cases want to guarantee that he will be physically incapable of hurting our community again.

"Expiation" and "atonement" are moral concepts, once generally discussed by legal and moral philosophers. Theoretically, the legally imposed suffering of convicted wrongdoers allowed their souls to escape their mutilated corpses and at least avoid the severer tortures of the damned in the hereafter. One whose ears were deafened by the approaching tread of the headsman's heavy foot probably drew scant comfort from having confessed his sins to, and received a blessing from, a priest with whom he did not agree.

Healing and reconciliation, as mutual and reciprocal covenants, are, perhaps more often than not, rendered impossible by the intransigence of one or even both parties to a social conflict. It is perhaps in resolution of this quandary that the community, through its lawfully appointed vicar, frequently bestows its blessing and insincere protestations of love upon a victim before the executioner lops off his head. In a less-than-perfect world, the community has healed itself by cutting off its offending member, choosing the pain and the scar over what it perceives to be a cancer.

At least some portions of the medical community are beginning to recognize surgery as a less-than-perfect last-ditch option where true healing has not taken place. It may be time to look at litigation the same way. No one thinks to ask a tumor, or a maimed leg, if *it* has been healed by its excision: by the same token, we cannot make the same inquiry of a Joan of Arc or an Ethel Rosenburg.

All too many American lawyers view justice as an unattainable and abstract goal, seeing themselves as specialized technicians with no responsibility for the whole; the flaws and imperfections of the system are deemed inevitable and acceptable, and, in the end, the daily pursuit of justice is regarded as a game in which they, as participants, are winners or losers.

We do not perceive our legal system as being a healing process. For instance, we speak of penal law—the law relating to execution of sentence on convicted criminals—as having four distinct and, in many cases, mutually exclusive goals: retribution (a modern term having something in common with the old concept of expiation), deterrence, sequestration, and rehabilitation, which also contains some of the ancient concept of "atonement." Theoretically (and *only* theoretically) our modern penal system accomplishes all four goals simultaneously. A wrongdoer is punished by putting him in a very nasty place for a long period of time, and society is somehow healed by knowing that he is "paying his debt" and receiving as much suffering as he inflicted upon his victim. In this process, through the intervention of counselors and by the passage of time and the opportunity to repent and meditate upon his wrongdoing, the wrongdoer is rehabilitated and emerges from incarceration a new person, reformed in thought and deed, and prepared to start afresh as a contributing member of society. During his period of incarceration, the as-yet unhealed felon is sequestered from society so that, until his debt has been paid and his recovery is complete, he is temporarily precluded from engaging in other wrongful acts. Finally, this entire process is so difficult and painful to the recovering, sequestered, and suffering wrongdoer that his unhappiness will set an example to others and deter them from wrongful acts.

Unfortunately, we don't really believe all that. Basically, we settle for what we can, retribution and sequestration. It is rare for the human animal to learn from the misfortune of his brother, because he assumes that he won't get caught, or that it won't happen to him: deterrence does not work. The number of released convicts who wind up back in jail lends credence to the opinion of many lawyers that prisons are the graduate schools of criminal behavior. In fact, those few sensitive and malleable enough to be reformed by the prison experience are those least likely to survive it: prisons are not centers of rehabilitation in our society.

The law cannot be, and in fact is not, "value free." Lawyers and the legal system cannot abdicate responsibility for adherence to moral and ethical principle. At the same time, attempts to embody morality within law can be harmful, and spiritually and politically stultifying. Like most theoretical constructs, the law, no matter how "moral," is only as good as the fallible human beings who implement it and bring it to life.

Present-day law seems to fail as a healing process on both the criminal and the so-called "civil" sides of the confrontation process between society and its individual members. The distinctions between "civil" and "criminal" law are being blurred by a combination of our society's complex self-perception, the decisions of courts, the behavior of law enforcement authorities, and the enactments of lawmakers. There are increasingly complex types and numbers of behavior that are perceived as criminal in our society, ranging from emotional abuse of children and the elderly to toxic waste discharge.

Was, for example, the near-destruction of the ecology of the Prince William Sound by the Exxon Corporation a crime? Many feel a crime was committed, but we are helpless to decide what human being was the criminal. Our community's desire to "get even" certainly led to the arrest, incarceration and conviction of Joseph Hazelwood, captain of the *Exxon Valdez*; but our society's equally strong sense of fairness and our reluctance to make one individual responsible for the wrongful acts of many led, almost as certainly, to the reversal of that conviction by the Alaska Supreme Court. It is no tribute to the lawyers involved in either prosecuting or defending the case, or the system itself, that the pain remains unhealed that was occasioned by the reckless endangerment of one of the most beautiful environments on the face of the Earth by a giant corporation and an equally uncaring government bureaucracy. The legal system did not fulfill its role in our community by abdicating its healing role; Hazelwood, his crowing to the contrary notwithstanding, has not been "exonerated"; and the Exxon Corporation's paying off thousands of fishermen and spending even more millions of dollars in self-eulogizing advertising, has not healed the wounds. Some cleanup efforts, coupled with the mighty regenerative powers of the Sound itself, have probably made great strides towards the restoration of that sensitive ecosystem. But somehow, the rest of us are waiting for it to happen again, having no assurance that Exxon will not continue using inadequate, paper-thin hulls, captained by inept alcoholics, under the "supervision" of uncaring and underpaid Coast Guardsmen, to create an even bigger tragedy in the future.

Certainly, there were lawyers enough involved. They flocked, in rapacious hordes, to Alaska to recruit clients with dreams of wealth. Meanwhile the Exxon Corporation bought or built entire office towers in Anchorage for their damage-control troops. Everybody made gobs of money off Exxon, which counted the game well played because it controlled and limited the amount it lost, and only this disempowered world—the rest of us—came out a loser. The healing and reconciling process simply did not work.

Our national love affair with law and lawyers, it seems, has failed to produce reconciliation and healing of the social ills with which the law is supposed to deal. Is this to suggest that the rapacity of corporations and Wall Street pirates and the drug-ridden criminal violence of our inner cities are the fault of our legal system? The law, after all, neither created not controls corner-cutting bean counters, Wall Street pirates, nor drug lords. I submit, however, that the law and lawyers voluntarily "enable" much of the lawful wrongness as well as the wrongful lawlessness of our society. In one of the many movies glorifying criminality in recent years, a criminal kingpin is advised by his legal "mouthpiece" that a proposed scheme is "illegal." The enraged capo successfully cows his lawyer by roaring at him, "I don't pay you to tell me it's illegal, I pay you to *make* it legal."

The law can serve as an instrument of healing and lawyers as healers only on an individual basis as a matter of individual choice, with all the difficulty and sacrifice implied thereby. I nonetheless believe that law, as an institution, can ease this choice and perform more readily its function in society by institutionally encouraging lawyers to perceive themselves as healers.

Many young lawyers view themselves as champions of the underdog, would-be "knights" whose sole goal is to right wrongs, redress grievances, and restore the balance of power. All too soon, however, they find themselves seeking power, either for their clients or, even worse, for themselves. When lawyers come to see themselves as healers, as makers-whole of that which has been broken, and legal institutions come to encourage and nurture that self-perception, things can change. Then, lawyers will no longer "keep score" and work from the universal mindset that for every winner there must be a loser. If more lawyers saw themselves in this way, they might see conflict as an opportunity for reconciliation, rather than victory.

Complete restoration of fractured social relationships may be as unattainable for law as a cure for cancer seems to be for medicine. But reconciliation and healing can be goals, however unattainable, and lawyers who perceive the law as a process of reconciliation can make a difference—small in individual instances, but massive in eventual application.

Redeeming the Holy Sparks
Evil, Healing, and the
Soul of the World

Eduardo Rauch

Every day is a god,
each day is a god,
and holiness holds forth in time....
      —Annie Dillard, *Holy the Firm*[1]

As we examine the history of the West in the last two thousand years it would seem that both the good and the evil we have done in the world have become deeper, more sophisticated, and more intense. There is something tragic and paradoxical about this situation, and certainly mysterious. If there were a logic to our psychological and spiritual natures, we would hope to discover that our human adventure has made progress toward a better world, in which life in all its dimensions is increasingly understood as sacred. Instead we seem to be heading simultaneously in opposing directions: While we have become able to empathize in amazing ways with multiple forms of life, we are also responsible for the European Holocaust, genocide in Cambodia, and more recently for the totally irrational fratricidal violence in the former Yugoslavia. We swim with dolphins and follow whales in order to listen to their songs, while we still murder each other in the most chilling and methodical of ways and destroy our natural world with irresponsible abandon. We are able to converse with the very stones that lie by the road and we carry on serious discussions about the legal rights of trees, while we firebomb the temporary homes of refugees in Germany, abandon Haitian exiles on the high seas, and permit violence against women and children to increase worldwide.

There is both doom and redemption in the air, and these days are at the same time dangerous and full of possibilities. Some people search for false messiahs, or seek refuge in authoritarian religions, while others look at all of this with a cynical eye and abandon the spiritual battlefield to pursue petty personal goals.

Nonetheless others still join the work in hospices for the terminally ill or struggle to save starving populations on the African continent. They work to salvage drug addicts in our inner city ghettos or to secure refuge for the tigers on the Indian subcontinent.

We must therefore ask: What is the difference between murderers and healers? Are we born to an implacable destiny? Are we made by our lives? Is God looking on? And if we were born for some purpose, can our destinies be saved or cursed by the efforts, the love, or the failure of our communities?

While attending Adolph Eichmann's trial in Jerusalem, Hannah Arendt wrote of being amazed when she became aware that the accused was a common, even simple man. And yet he had been molded into one of the great murderers in history, having become one of the main architects of the extermination of European Jewry. Under different circumstances perhaps Eichmann would have become an anonymous shopkeeper. Or would he? In Sarajevo, young men who started out repairing cars or planting potatoes became with amazing ease members of militia groups who systematically murdered their neighbors in cold blood. If a charismatic preacher had come to their towns, would these young men have equally joined the forces of some form of God, or some utopian community?

It is frightening to consider the possibility that we are so malleable, so easily swayed, so cheaply transformed. We want to—we need to—believe that there is a more solid core to our being, a destiny more under our control, a quality of being that comes to us from some sacred and unknown territory which can guide us through the treacherous moral challenges of the human condition.

It is the question of good and evil which poses itself, a question which has never been answered satisfactorily. In our time evil is sometimes understood as illness, the result of circumstances related to our family lives and other interpersonal histories. Yesterday, if we had committed certain crimes, we would have been hanged for them; today for the same crimes we might be sent to the psychiatric ward.[2] Sometimes God is seen as the source of both good and evil; at other times evil is seen to be independent from Him. Some religions argue for a measure of free will, saying we can choose our own path, yet we cannot avoid being the victims of mistakes, temptation, or accident. Moreover, evil is not always defined as negative. In some religious systems, evil and misfortune are seen either as a purifying force—the impulse for creation and procreation, as a punishment—or as a necessary challenge for the growth and evolution of the soul.

In Judaism, according to some of its mystical doctrines, evil was brought into the world at the very beginning when God created the cosmos out of His own being. Some Jewish theologians see the entrance of evil into our world as an accident in which vessels containing the holy light of creation were shattered, dispersing sparks of holiness into the material world, where they are now trapped in husks of matter and from where they must be redeemed. That is the function of the human race; to return these sparks into God's realm and thus restore the original perfection. This is *Tikkun Olam*, one of the bases for free will. Without evil in the world we would be unable to choose. There is another Jewish view about the source of evil: it was already part of the original holy lights and the shattering of the vessels containing that light was an intentional act whose very purpose was to bring evil into the world. This view of the dual nature of God, that He is responsible for both good and evil, has not always been easily accepted by some Jewish thinkers.

In either case, whether evil came into the world by accident or divine intention, the role of the human race is to perform *Tikkun Olam*, to repair the world, to heal it, to redeem the cosmos from its fallen state. This task is performed by restituting the scattered and exiled sparks to their higher abode through acts of goodness as defined by Jewish law, and by struggling against the general evil in the world. *Shekhina*, the feminine face of God, is also seen by some as falling into the material realm when the vessels break. She is often called Mother Earth and finds herself in exile. To lead the *Shekhina* back to God is the true purpose of the Torah. The most powerful actions that can help achieve that goal are both prayer and living by the commandments of the Torah.

Later mystical philosophies of Judaism, such as Habad (an eighteenth-century branch of the Hasidic movement), put much more weight on the dialectic between spiritualism and activism and on the interplay between mystical interests and social-ethical concerns. Humanity is called to *yihud* (unification) with God in His realm in an effort to transcend the boundaries of existence, time and space, while drawing the divinity into the lower realms, making It dwell in the world. At the same time, paradoxically, Habad philosophy, with views of evil similar to those of earlier forms of Jewish mysticism, argues that the whole cosmos is made of the divine, there *is* only God. For God, our material world is no more than an illusion, and yet it is one to which we must dedicate ourselves with all our being while we live in it, both straining to reach the Godhead and bringing goodness into our Home.

Habad philosophy is imbued with a dynamism which many earlier mystical philosophies lacked. The processes of making the world and transcending it, of bringing *Tikkun* and going beyond the material, are all occurring in the now. They are ongoing, indispensable phenomena, and bestow enormous responsibilities on each one of us. Thus God is in the process of becoming just as we are, and the dynamics of healing and self-revelation run both from earth to heaven and from heaven to earth.

※

To talk about healing in our contemporary world is to be over-whelmed. There is so much pain, so much violence, so much despair. Levels of injustice, mass murder, and oppression are at an all-time high, and the destruction of our natural world proceeds at a frenetic pace despite the efforts of enlightened and well-intentioned activists the world over. How can we participate in the process of healing; what does it mean to heal? To choose among all our tragedies can make us feel selfish—would that mean we do not care about every-thing else? And yet we must choose.

Heroes and true healers are almost always local; they perform in small settings, often anonymously. Their work of redemption is done with such modesty that often they themselves are unaware of the sig-nificance of their actions. Such is the case for example with Christians who saved Jews by hiding them during the Nazi persecu-tion. When questioned about their actions, which clearly put them in mortal danger, they invariably responded that they did what they had to do and that there hadn't been any choice in the matter.

When we are witnesses to healing our hearts know it. We are moved—after the event we find ourselves someplace else. The world is not the same, even if the encounter only involves two people, or if a man pulls out a thorn from a lion's paw. *Tikkun Olam* has taken place, a holy spark thus freed from its earthly dwelling travels to the Godhead. Someplace on earth, pain has been diminished, an encounter has crystalized, and *yihud* in the higher and lower realms has occurred.

I recall a story by Saint-Exupery in which a few miners are trapped in a mineshaft. In the process of attempting to save the miners' lives, many members of the salvage crew die. Despite what appears to be a mixed blessing we are all healed by such an act, and we join in the accomplishment of the few. Rescue and sacrifice are elements of a sacred geometry we can all recognize.

And yet most healing occurs quietly, almost secretly, in circum-stances that will only be known to the participants. In this world of constant flow, of eternal change, much needs to be saved, healed, redeemed, elevated. And that can only come through interactions between people, between people and the spiritual realm, between people and animals, between people and the so-called inanimate world.

Walk down the street of a busy city amidst the chaos of traffic, the implacable noise of vehicle and machine, the unrelenting pace of people heading to infinite destinations. Suddenly you see a blind man and his black labrador guide dog. They advance as one amid the formlessness and the indifference of our sidewalk disarray. The dog, attentive to every move, makes his way among a thousand targets. His pace is cautious but firm, neither too fast nor too slow, always aware of his master's progress. There is a wisdom in the animal's actions that goes well beyond our comprehension. His patience is inexhaustible, his caring of the utmost seriousness, his concentration on the details and nuances of his work painstakingly intense. Occasionally the dog will turn his head to read his master's intentions, to capture his need, and then resume his discipline. As dog and man turn a corner, they disappear from our view.

There will be those who will ascribe the dog's behavior to training, or to instinct, or to the mechanisms of an essentially static Cartesian nature. Training helps and the dog must have some natural skills, but after all is said we can only awaken what is already there, whatever the essence of dogness brings into the world. If our vision is limited to some mechanistic view of the world, everything will be necessarily reduced to cold explanations based on a simple-minded and now old-fashioned science. Until recently most human behavior was explained in the same way.

Our world has been radically *desouled*, it has lost its life, its independent vitality. At best we still believe in our own souls. If we seek it, the soul of the world shows herself most immediately with the presence of everyday things. It is there that we can become ecstatically one with a hyacinth, or suffer the injuries of a polluted river in our own being. We can be surprised by holiness, by the holy sparks hidden in husks of matter, overcome by the divine nature of things.

The twentieth-century Jewish philosopher Martin Buber argued that the divine could only be engaged through deep encounters between people, creatures, and all other things of our world. He called these encounters "I-Thou" relationships, rather than barren "I-it" meetings, in which the spirits of the parties have failed to touch each other, and thus have weakened both the world and God. Although Buber in his later philosophy rejected the mystical fusion of the parties in the encounter, the power of the Buberian encounter is no less impressive. In the following story Buber recounts an experience of his boyhood: "When I was eleven years of age, spending the summer on my grandparents' estate, I used, as often as I could do it unobserved, to steal into the stable and gently stroke the neck of my darling, a broad dapple-gray horse. It was not a casual delight but a great, certainly friendly, but also deeply stirring happening. If I am to explain it now, beginning from the still very fresh memory of my hand, I must say that what I experienced in touch with the animal was the Other, the immense otherness of the Other, which however did not remain strange like the otherness of the ox and ram, but rather let me draw near and touch it. When I stroked the mighty mane, sometimes marvelously smooth-combed, at other times just as astonishingly wild, and felt the life beneath my hand, it was as though the element of vitality itself bordered on my skin, something that was not I, was certainly not akin to me, palpably the other, not just another, really the Other itself; and yet it let me approach, confided itself to me, placed itself elementally in the relation of Thou and Thou with me."[3]

As we have seen, the experience of catharsis and healing doesn't necessarily occur through what we generally define as positive experiences. Bernie Siegel talks about the healing that can take place even in our dying. At the end of a long fatal illness, when a person comes to terms with his condition, when he has said his last goodbyes, death can be a welcome release. It is paradoxically a form of healing, even if initially we might feel outraged by the idea.

To become healed and to be able to heal can be the consequence of wounds we have suffered that we still carry with us. Life experiences might hurt us deeply and yet awaken us from a slumber, make us whole, help us see the world in all its painstaking richness. Even if we carry the wound for life, it is through pained perception of the world that we come to embody and radiate a depth of feeling and empathy which permits us to heal others. It is in such ways that the wounded healer is born. Shattered, not unlike the original vessels of creation, the wounded healer carries within him both the tragic memory of that cosmic disaster and a powerful awareness of the sacredness of all life.

NOTES
1. Annie Dillard, *Holy the Firm* (New York: Harper & Row, 1977), p.40.
2. Good and evil also change in our perceptions as consciousness evolves. Once slavery was a socially accepted institution. The genocide of Native Americans by European colonizers was hardly seen as a tragedy in the old continent except by very special souls such as that of Bartolome de Las Casas (1474-1566), an early Spanish historian and Dominican missionary in the Americas who was the first to expose the tragedy and called for the abolition of Native American slavery.
3. Martin Buber, *Meetings* (La Salle, Ill.: Open Court Publishing Co., 1973), p.26.

The Alchemy of Illness

Kat Duff

*In 1988, the author developed chronic fatigue and immune dys-
function syndrome (CFIDS), an illness best described as a bad flu
that never goes away. As the only remedy is prolonged rest, she
spent nearly two years in bed, during which time she reflected on
the function and purpose of illness.*

After I had been sick for several months, it became clear to me that I
was changing in fundamental ways and that I would never go back to
my "old self." One day, when I was taking my morning walk across the
mesa, I heard myself muttering under my breath, over and over like a
droning chant, "I don't know who I am anymore. I don't know who I
am anymore." Like many sick people, I had begun to realize that my
illness was not so much a state of being as a process of transformation.
My body was changing, losing weight, luster, and vitality, while
assuming an ethereal tenor, just as my interests and preferences were
shifting dramatically. I yearned for some kind of map or diagram that
could describe, and even predict, these strange mutations of character
I felt myself undergoing.

Then one day, as I stood in my kitchen stirring powdered vitamin
C into a glass of water, staring at the vast array of medicinal bottles

on the counter, I realized that my illness and its healing were a matter of chemistry. That chemistry was very physical, as in the magnesium and potassium I took to help my body assimilate the vitamin C, but there was something more to it, for there were times when remedies worked, or did not work, for no apparent reason. For example, I often felt better as soon as I swallowed my vitamin C, long before it had time to take effect. Medical researchers call it the "placebo effect"; I prefer to call it magic, for it occurs when something—a pill or a word—is imbued with power and meaning, and so becomes more effective. That is alchemy.

Like many schooled in the scientific worldview, I once had the impression that the alchemists of medieval and Renaissance Europe were misguided fools at best, greedy charlatans at worst, who tried to turn lead into gold in secret laboratories. While some may have been just that, many were astute observers of the transformations that occur in visible and invisible realms; their experiments form the basis of modern chemistry and homeopathy, while informing the practice of modern psychotherapy and astrology. Carl Jung was among the first in this century to revive their teachings; he and his followers inter-preted their arcane formulas metaphorically, which was the mode of thought at that time, and so made their enormous insights available to us.[1] Under Jung's keen perception, alchemy emerged as an eloquent model of the stages and processes of spiritual evolution—one which has offered me much-needed comfort and guidance in coping with the vicissitudes of illness.

One of the central tenets of alchemical philosophy was that physi-cal decay is the beginning of the "Great Work": spiritual transforma-tion. Paracelsus, a renowned physician and alchemist of the sixteenth century, wrote: "Decay is the beginning of all birth...the midwife of very great things!" adding that this is "the deepest mystery and mira-cle that He [God] has revealed to mortal man."[2] People who have endured great physical trauma—car accidents, war injuries, surgery, or torture—occasionally bear witness to this mystery with stories of tun-nels of light, angelic presences, and religious conversions. Physical pain cancels the claims of the world and the hold of ordinary con-sciousness, opening us to the unworldly forces of the metaphysical.

46

No wonder the image of Jesus suffering on the cross is the central symbol of spiritual rebirth in Christianity.

Alchemists began the Great Work of spiritual transformation with what they called *prima materia*, the basic matter or problem. In their efforts to make gold, they did not start with refined or precious metals, such as silver or copper, but with the most common, base, and ugly of metals: lead. In psychological terms, this means the work of spiritual transformation springs from the places we feel most inferior or debased. Alchemists outlined four qualities that can help us to find and identify this ever-so-promising matter: (1) It is ordinary and found everywhere; (2) people are often revolted by it; (3) it has many names and faces but only one essence; (4) it is boundless, consuming, and overwhelming. In summary, *prima materia* is that which is everywhere, unavoidable, despicable, and out of control in our lives: the diseases of our bodies and souls. Is it any wonder that many Renaissance physicians were also alchemists?

Alchemists put this bothersome matter into a closed container and cooked it; it is important to note that they did not add or subtract anything, but simply dissolved the matter in its own water. In so doing, they amplified the distress, until the matter transformed of its own accord, in the recognition that healing is derived from the illness itself. Paracelsus explained that each disease "bears its own remedy within itself.... Health must grow from the same root as disease."[3] This understanding forms the basis for the homeopathic practice of treating like with like. It is also echoed in the words of many sick people who discover, after searching in vain for a cure, that the answers cannot be found outside oneself; they must come from within.

The alchemists insisted that two things must happen before the cure can be extracted from the disease: the problem must be kept in a closed container, and it must be reduced to its original state through a process of breakdown. The limitations and immobility of illness provide the closed container that enables this transformation, precisely because there is no way out. Early on in my illness my dreams offered the image of a snarl of snakes stuck in a bottle for my situation; alchemical texts are filled with images of dangerous animals—lions or wolves—trapped in the chemist's flask. Alice James called herself "bottled lightning…a geyser of emotions, sensations, speculations, and reflections fermenting…in my poor old carcass" when she was dying of cancer.[4] The isolation and lack of sympathy or understanding that sick people often endure may even be necessary to secure the walls of the container, so that nothing is spilt or shared, and the matter inside will reach the point of transmutation. The walled space of illness, like therapy, intensifies the brooding and incubates the egg.

Most religious traditions actually prescribe the disciplines that illnesses impose—abstinence, isolation, and stillness—creating artificial walled spaces for the purposes of spiritual development. The Asclepian temples of ancient Greece contained private incubation chambers where sick people would lie down, drift into an altered state of twilight sleep, and receive the ministrations of the healing gods and goddesses; could it be that we are more amenable to their touch in a place of stillness and isolation? Whether confined by the small circle of a sweat lodge, the four walls of a monk's cell, or the four posts of the sickbed, the mind cannot be distracted by the tasks of movement, and so turns back upon itself, in the downward, inward spiral of a whirlpool. While at first I often feel trapped, and sometimes panic for fear of losing my mind, I inevitably come to cherish the immense sense of leisure and inner spaciousness I discover when freed from drive and desire.

Much as sick people complain, often vociferously, about their isolation and the lack of sympathy from others (we constantly switch doctors and friends in search of the "good ear"), many come to recognize that this invisible wall between the sick and the well protects both. Laura Chester wrote that "the isolation of illness did not seem to be a bad thing," for she was "left alone to revive the inner seed, which had withered under the intensity of interaction."[5] There came a point in the depths of my illness when I realized that the people closest to me could no longer bear to hear of my despair, which was inconsolable; it seemed to short-circuit their capacities for attention and compassion. After a long night of self-confrontation, I decided to keep that bitter nest of despair to myself from then on—and a curious shift occurred. While I felt scared, like a lost child whose cries could not be heard, I also felt infused with power, a power I associate with mountain climbers and deep-sea divers, people who face their destinies and know their survivals rest in their own two hands. I felt, to use Chester's words, "my soul opening and strengthening, like a muscle."

In the closed container of the alchemist's flask, the problem is reduced, broken down, and returned to its original state of disorder, which the alchemists termed *massa confusa*, meaning confused mass. What has been learned under the assumptions of health must be unlearned under the exigencies of disease. Sick people often speak of peeling back the layers of a lifetime like an onion, for the deepest parts of ourselves are also the oldest. Homeopathists and acupuncturists point out that in healing we work back through every illness we have had, in reverse order, until we eventually arrive at the root, which may be variously described as a genetic inclination, a predilection of character, one's karma or destiny. These origins are almost too profound and ethereal to identify, except in the altered states of illness.

Alchemists identified many processes that facilitate this breakdown: loss of composure and return to origins. Four of the most basic ones—*calcinatio* (burning by fire), *solutio* (dissolving in water), *sublimatio* (rising in air), and *coagulatio* (falling into earth)—were associated with the elements of fire, water, air, and earth, which are so evident in illness. While these processes were often described as stages, they do not occur in any particular sequence; we slip in and out of them, back and forth among them, spending more time in some than others, according to our temperamental inclinations, and the requirement of our souls.

Calcinatio is a burning process most evident in fevers, but it is also associated with the intensity of frustrated desires. How many times have we heard ourselves say, "I'm burning up inside," or "she's burning" with anger, resentment, or envy? There is no doubt about it, we cannot get much of what we want—sleep, pleasure, activity, or company—when we are sick, and we rarely manage to accommodate ourselves to these losses. We are impossibly frustrated every night we cannot sleep, angry every time we cannot go out, envious when our friends go off skiing, resentful when they eat the foods forbidden to us. This struggle is the burning of *calcinatio*, and one is quickly reminded that passions are their own punishment, as the Buddhists claim.

49

Alchemical texts assert that the process of *calcinatio* produces salt, which manifests as bitterness, until it is further purified into wisdom. This observation makes me wonder whether the interventions of modern medicine lock us into bitterness and keep us from the promise of wisdom by intercepting the disease process, which is also, in alchemical terms, the process of enlightenment. Illnesses have their own timing; as John Donne observed, "a sickness must ripen of itself, [we] cannot hasten it."[6]

Solutio is a dissolving process that melts walls and rigidities, opening us up to the full chaos and mystery of life, often with a great surge of emotion. This process usually starts with a sense of confusion or disorientation; sick people often wander into strange rooms at all hours of day and night, only to stop with startled looks, as if to ask, "What am I doing here?" Standing with furrowed brows, we may hear the clock ticking, see shadows cast by a streetlight, and feel a dampness in the air, but not know what any of it means. Emotions catch in our throats and tears are common under the sway of *solutio*, tears of frustration or unexpected relief, sorrow, or joy. There are moments of great fear, when shadows assume demonic shapes, but there are also times of euphoria, when the tinkles of chandeliers become the voices of angels.

In the process of *sublimatio* we rise, like smoke from a fire, above ourselves to assume a more remote, encompassing vision; some would call it disassociation or leaving one's body. *Sublimatio* is a transcendence, a journey to higher realms, and it offers extraordinary revelations. Moments like these help us to disidentify from our bruised and burning bodies, enabling us to escape the suffering temporarily; the visions they inspire ultimately help us to endure and redeem that suffering.

The last alchemical operation, *coagulatio*, is quite evident in illness. It relates to the element of earth and represents the ways in which we are confined or bound by physical existence, by the necessities of our bodies and souls. Under the pressure and coercion of disease, we lose the spaciousness, freedom, and ease we had come to assume in health; here we encounter the fierce limits of our destinies, limits we have not chosen but must endure and be shaped by. A painter friend of mine, who has developed rheumatoid arthritis in recent years, can work only on her good days because her fingers are so swollen and gnarled with pain. She used to paint huge sweeping canvases; now she paints miniatures.

All four processes of breakdown—*calcinatio, solutio, sublimatio,* and *coagulatio*—end in *mortificatio,* meaning decay or death-making, one of the most important stages of the alchemical process; in fact, it is the bottom, the critical turning point of the entire labor. *Mortificatio,* which is also known as the *nigredo,* or blackening, is the experience of defeat, failure, and humiliation, which the disabilities and dependencies of illness certainly inspire. The process was often pictured in alchemical texts as an old king, or a young innocent, laid out on his deathbed, images that have popped up regularly in my dreams since I developed CFIDS. To the extent that we derive our self-worth from our abilities, our aspirations, or the appearances we maintain, we are "mortified" by their loss in the devastations of illness. We feel beaten, ground down, and crushed by the unending series of small failures— the missed deadlines, spilled food, and unkind remarks. One of the most difficult things I have had to deal with in my illness is the fact that I could no longer reliably do the quality of work I had come to expect of myself.

There came a point in my illness, just as I was starting to get a little more energy back, when I fell into a state of intense despair and could not get out of it, much to my fright and shame. At first I blamed it on my illness, which is known to cause neurological disturbances, but eventually I realized that it was *my* depression, even if it was triggered by CFIDS, that I had seen it before and would probably see it again, and that it was up to me to figure out how to come to terms with it. I felt small, dirty, and tainted by my own faultiness, but on the other hand, something in me thrilled to the challenge of cracking this nut, of chewing the gristle, simply because it was mine to crack and chew. I decided to stop complaining and just sit with my dirt.

My dreams became unusually lucid, like open palms divulging their secrets, giving me clear advice. They told me that hatred is not to be avoided or indulged, but offered back to the powers of the deep, for their own inscrutable purposes; that faith is not something you must have or cannot lose, but something you practice because the world depends on it. I started making daily prayers, and though I fumbled with inexperience, they helped. One of my dreams encouraged me to make a place for my pack of black dogs—my despair, envy, and hate—at the end of my bed.

Perhaps there was also a dog by the name of greed, for in another dream I could not get gas for my car until I admitted my greed. That was difficult, for greed is a quality I detest in others, but eventually I found the part of myself that wants it all for myself, the part of me that secretly hoards ice cream, books, and money. Then my dream took an interesting turn: When the gas station attendant put gas in my car, I realized that I needed my greed, in the form of strong, selfish desires, in order to get going! So when a naturopath offered me a homeopathic remedy for serotonin (one of the neurotransmitters that affects mood, which is commonly disturbed by CFIDS), I took it greedily, and within a few days the shell of my despair cracked.

I do not know whether it was the serotonin remedy that dispelled my despair or the fact that I had to eat my shadow and claim my greed in order to take it; perhaps these seemingly separate events were simultaneous reflections in the mirrors of my body and soul. Herein lies one of the keynotes of alchemical philosophy: that all things are related to their opposites, and the goal, whether it be known as spiritual revelation, self-realization, or healing, always involves the reunion of opposites.

Now that I am—hopefully—through the worst of it, I feel very lucky and eternally grateful for the hands that helped me through those straits to reclaim some lost parts of myself. I cannot forget that those places and my capacity to choose them exist within me, nor can I forget what I have learned about my own fragility and that of the world, so the prayers continue. At the same time, I feel more solid, as though finally standing on both my feet for the first time in my life, as if the pale outline of myself had at last been filled in with color. This combination of fragility and strength is just one of the many curious contradictions that come true in the midst of illness. As the alchemists often said, the "sun and its shadow" complete the work.

As we accept the shadow, we are naturally humbled. Hubris, which translates as going "beyond the allotted portion," our so-human desire to push our limits and feel powerful, is slain in illness, to nurture reverence and humility, the simple recognition of our human littleness in relation to a greater Mystery. Disease, defeat, and the humility they inspire, actually constellate the numinous powers of nature and the soul, just as the vast expanses of sea, sky, or canyon cliffs call forth our awe.

In alchemical terms, base matter is transmuted through the process of death into gold, the philosopher's stone, the self-realization that heals all by combining opposites and rectifying one-sidedness. Illness operates upon the stuff of our bodies to reveal and release that spiritual essence—our unique natures, powers, and virtues—which lies buried in the body "like a mummy in the tomb," to quote Paracelsus. It is a process of development that just carries "to its end something that has not yet been completed," as the alchemists often insisted.

Not long ago, when I turned down an invitation to attend a Buddhist meditation retreat because I was not well enough to sit upright for hours, I felt sad, wondering when I would be able to resume spiritual practices. Then, as I was falling asleep that night, it occurred to me that my illness is my spiritual path and practice—at least for now.

NOTES
1. See Carl Jung, *Psychology and Alchemy*, vol. 12, *The Collected Works of* C.G. *Jung*, The Bollingen Series XX (Princeton: Princeton University Press, 1953); Edward F. Edinger, *Anatomy of the Psyche* (La Salle, Ill.: Open Court Publishing Co., 1985); Liz Greene, "Alchemical Symbolism in the Horoscope," in Greene and Sasportas, *Dynamics of the Unconscious* (York Beach, Maine: Samuel Weiser, 1988); Charles Ponce, *Alchemy* (Berkeley, Calif.: North Atlantic Books, 1983); and Marie-Louise von Franz, *Alchemical Imagination* (Dallas: Spring Publications, 1979).
2. Paracelsus, *Selected Writings*, Jolande Jacobi, ed., Norbert Guterman, tr. (New York: Princeton University Press, 1951), pp. 143-44.
3. *Ibid.*, p. 78.
4. Alice James, *The Diary of Alice James*, Leon Edel, ed. and intro. (New York: Dodd, Mead & Co., 1964), p. 25.
5. Laura Chester, *Lupus Novice* (Berryton, N.Y.: Station Hill Press, 1987), p. 50.
6. John Donne, "Devotions," in *Complete Poetry and Selected Works of John Donne and Complete Poetry of William Blake* (New York: Random House, 1941), p. 335.

Flowers

Ruth Rudner

The Atlantic beats against the ancient granite cliffs rising straight and high and dark along the Maine Coast. It is as if the continent itself were walled in, defended from the relentless force that would pull its land back into the sea. Exploding in roiling white spume against the rocks, the Atlantic pours over them to fall back in foam on the green edge of ocean. The spray shoots cliff-top high to lie in sea drops on our arms and lips and the black rock on which we stand. Lower down, the water glides over glossy, ocean-smoothed rock into dark and glistening pools. Where rock wall and ocean meet, rough waves surge into a narrow rock canyon. Trapped, they blast upward, spouting geyser-like into the sea air. Spouting Horn, this place is called. It is high tide. There is a wind, a rough sea; in the distance, a sailboat with lowered sails.

You believe you have some kind of power because you stand above the sea and observe. Then you taste the sea on your lips and you remember it and you know that, to the sea, you are nothing. The sea gives. The sea takes back. The land and all its life are temporary. On loan. Not to be taken for granted.

Spouting Horn is one of those places on Earth where it is perfectly clear there is no alternative to Nature; where its force, the force of

54

oceans, of gathering storms, of tides and time offering neither succor nor consolation, presents to us the fierce insistence of eternity. In the waxing and waning of tides is the whole story of life.

A twenty-minute walk from the ocean, on the inlet at Tenant's Harbor, Blueberry Cove Camp nestles in a gentle landscape, a place where meadow has been carved from the forest sloping down to the inlet. The inlet curves around Blueberry Cove. At low tide you can practically walk across it to the town of Tenant's Harbor without getting your feet wet. Tenant's Harbor is one of those old Maine towns with big 18th-century clapboard houses that look wonderful on picture postcards. Old Maine. Old New England. Quiet, serious, hard, strong, thrifty, steadfast, unwavering, quintessential America.

The camp, on the other hand, represents a kind of revolution. Not that revolution isn't as basically American as clapboard houses and parsimonious speech. It's just that, in this particular landscape, you don't see it a whole lot.

Founded in 1949 by Henry and Bess Haskell, Blueberry Cove Camp was the first for-profit interracial camp in the country. The Haskells believed so fully in the rightness of integration that they staked their livelihood on it. They also believed that if they could show integration as a money-maker, others would follow their example. Although the camp caused a certain initial discomfort among the old guard Maine residents, in time, they incorporated it into their lives. Still, revolution is not a one-shot deal. Either it begets revolution or it is nothing more than the status quo in the hands of somebody else. Change isn't revolution. Change is just change.

Painter Jon Moscartelo of the Blueberry Cove Foundation (and himself a former camper) approached Joe Mondello and Bruce Detrick of the Tamarand Foundation in New York City with the idea of offering a weeklong camp at Blueberry Cove for families with HIV-positive children. For the Tamarand Foundation, whose mission is to bring nature and art to hospitals and to homes for children with AIDS, the camp offered the ideal, a chance to bring the children to nature instead of the other way around. The basic tenet of the Tamarand Foundation (named for Joe's six-month-old niece, Tamara, who died of AIDS, as did her mother, who was infected through a transfusion) is that life is nurtured by life. As Bruce says, "The spirit may be whole though the body is ill." For Henry Haskell, who is now in his 80s, and who lives down the road from the camp, the HIV camp—even though it was definitely not for profit—seemed a logical continuation of his work: In 1992, people's ignorance about those infected with HIV or AIDS is about on a par with their 1949 prejudices against blacks.

The timing of my first trip east in seven years coincided with the week of the camp. Bruce, who is my close, old friend, suggested that if I came up, I could help. Believing with all my heart in the work of the Tamarand Foundation, I had wanted to be of use for a long time, but there was little I could do from Montana. Blueberry Cove seemed an opportunity to help in the work, and do a favor for friends as well.

Bruce, Joe, and I arrived at Blueberry Cove two nights before the beginning of camp. Parking the car in the fog that had been with us the whole trip up from New York, we entered the main lodge where Jon and the regular camp staff waited for us in front of a warm fire. Coming to a new place on a foggy night, when you cannot see where you are, is disorienting. You move through darkness to come to a place you have never been. In spite of the warm fire, it has no reference points. You know that everything will be different in the morning, but morning is too far away to be of much use.

Yet, morning comes. In clear, bright day, without even the memory of fog, the camp director showed me the walk to the ocean. Following a dirt road lined with asters, blueberries, and swamp maples, we passed a corner where a domestic garden marked the side road to someone's house. The garden was well tended, a mass of vibrant flowers, their colors doubly vivid in the midst of the dense and tangled greens backing away from the road, and the small, subtle flowers and berries that grow wild on this granite land. Coming upon the garden was like entering a sudden moment of light in a dark forest. The light is lovely, a gift, but it is temporary, the vision of a moment. When, one day, the garden is no longer tended, those flowers will be displaced by what is wild, what is natural to this particular piece of earth, what works here on its own. With the exception of the ocean, it takes a kind of subtlety to survive in this landscape. How different from the Rocky Mountains with their flamboyant wildflowers, although maybe in all that space, flamboyance is required to make a point. Here, on granite, closed in by greenery, it is enough just to grow.

About three-quarters of a mile up the road, we entered forest, its floor covered by dogwood and reindeer moss, a deep green and silent place. I forgot we were walking to the ocean until, suddenly, it was all there was ahead of us, steel-blue, white-capped, stretching from us to the sky. We stood on high rock headlands at the edge of America, the Atlantic crashing full force a hundred feet below.

By the time the campers and most of the staff arrived on buses that brought them up from Providence and Boston, New York and New Jersey, Blueberry Cove felt familiar to me. Most of the thirteen families were black; two were Hispanic; one was white. What all of them shared was the fact of a child, or children, with HIV. Some children arrived with HIV-infected mothers; others with foster mothers or aunts because their mothers had died of AIDS, and with older siblings, children free of the infection. Besides cooks and a nurse with a direct line to AIDS pediatricians, the staff included musicians, naturalists, storytellers and, from Columbia Teachers' College, an artist and a dancer. The idea of the camp was to offer a little time out, a place to play, a safe haven where nature, art, and music could provide a supportive and healing environment.

Healing. The dictionary says it means "to make sound; to cure of disease or affliction." Yet, even where curing of disease cannot happen, healing is possible. The aching heart can become whole. Any aching heart.

The campers, city people all, were led to primitive cabins, some without electricity, none with anything more than beds and perhaps a shelf or rough table. A few showers and bathrooms are scattered throughout the camp.

We had put a vase of wildflowers in each cabin, but nobody seemed to notice in the rush to change cabins because this one was too small or too dark or too lonely. The sorting, the unpacking, the moving in and out and in went on late into the night. When the campers interrupted their settling in to pour into the lodge for dinner, there seemed so many of them: tiny children and slightly older children, women carrying babies, a few teenage girls, some large boys. I sat at a table with Karen, her three-year-old, Ty, her seventeen-year-old foster daughter, Dee Dee, her friend Wanda, Wanda's five-year-old nephew, Justin. Because I had already spent a little time with Karen and Wanda, I felt some familiarity. But I felt an intruder, too: the white woman, the staff person, the outsider.

At the staff meeting called for 11:00 p.m., the first free moment, no one else seemed to share that feeling. At first I wondered if I had been in Montana for so long that the diversity of the East had become foreign to me. Yet, the staff was also a mixture of races and backgrounds and I was not an "outsider" with them. Was it simply guilt at being healthy in the face of so much illness? Guilt at being—so far—lucky? If that was so, why did the rest of the staff not feel it? How were they able just to launch into their plans for the week? Yet, what else could they do? Dwelling on the unfairness of life was hardly to the point. Even I know that. I tried to tell myself it was merely late. I was tired. I had had no experience with such a project.

It was a relief, after the meeting, to walk down through the woods to the tent where I was camped, a relief to be alone. Sleeping on the ground in the woods was familiar. I always know where I am in the woods. The tent, out of sight of the camp buildings, provided me a privacy, a place that was my own. I treasured that place. Mornings, I woke to a view of forest ending at the inlet below; of tall, thin birches swaying in the wind, their shimmering leaves casting light that moved like water; of water in the inlet rippling against the shore, dappling the light that fell on it like quivering leaves. Now, at night, the tall shapes of trees reached into stars. I could hear the water swashing against the beach, and the ringing of the harbor buoys.

After breakfast the entire camp met to discuss the day—according to Blueberry Cove custom—in a circle on the grass. On this first morning, as on my own first morning, the confusion of the previous night was gone. There was a sense that everybody had moved in, the journey from fog unto morning repeated over and over. Small children and babies and the two Nubian goats that had the run of camp all walked around inside the circle.

Folksinger Nancy Mattila passed a smudgepot around the circle, offering its smoke to the Great Spirit as we all chanted, "The Earth is our mother, we must take care of her. Hey yanna, ho yanna, hey yanna . . ." Over and over we chanted as the smudgepot passed from hands to hands. A few of the children were self-conscious about lifting the pot and refused. Others did it shyly. The mothers and aunts lifted it for the littlest ones, their hands over the little hands so that even the babies could take part. Afterward, storyteller Christine Campbell, weaving a story out of all the threads that had come together in this place, presented us a common ground so that none of us were outsiders anymore. Nothing that happened in the circle, the interjection of a child, the sudden appearance overhead of an osprey, was left out of the story. In the soft Jamaican accent that filtered through all her plethora of voices, she incorporated the new into the familiar, offering us something magical, yet wholly believable. Magic. Truth. The right combination of outlooks to get through life, however long or short life turns out to be. It translates life to usable time, to the immediate moment. Allowing us to look at what is terrifying and come to resolution, it provides a context we can enter.

This is also what nature does, which is why using nature as a healer works. In nature, life goes from season to season, continuing forever. Even under the most adverse circumstances—a killer hurricane or unstoppable wildfire, earthquake, landslide, erupting volcano—the Earth picks up again and starts anew. The new life forms may differ from the old, but the change they represent is the essence of life. I saw it happen in Yellowstone Park after the fires of 1988 when the black earth of burned forests suddenly exploded with color—the gorgeous fuchsia flowers of fireweed and the brilliant yellow of arnica. What joy the earth presented then!

Flowers. Wildflowers. Garden flowers. They form a connection between one form of life and the next. Intermediaries, go-betweens, they are like angels. Children recognize angels. Some children probably are angels. As we chanted in the circle, Jo-Jo, who is not yet two, picked a yellow dandelion from the grass and brought it to me. I put it in my hair. "Look, he's flirting with her," his mother said to her friend. He took the dandelion from my hair and walked away with it, his baseball cap askew. Later, he came back and put his baseball cap on my head.

That evening Jo-Jo's mother had an asthma attack and, in the morning, decided to return home. Dee Dee brought Jo-Jo to breakfast while his mother packed. After Dee Dee fed Jo-Jo, I took him so she could eat. He was perfectly willing to be held by me. He had just come out of the hospital. There must have been so many strangers holding him in his life.

I showed him a bucket of cut flowers next to the breakfast table; first a huge yellow black-eyed susan at which he simply looked, then an equally huge fuchsia flower. He reached out to this one, touching it as if it were his mother's face.

On a walk to Henry Haskell's house to pick blueberries, Ty, who had been sent along even though he wanted to go with Dee Dee to a place at tide's edge too dangerous for the youngest children, sulked much of the way. The others, a dozen small black children running along the edges of perfect yards fronting large New England houses, were curious about everything. Only Ty, his arms just stretching around the huge berry bucket he insisted on carrying, seemed to look at nothing. He remained entirely inside himself until we came upon a pair of enormous wooden wheels in a yard—some gigantic old wagon hitch—eight feet high. He walked over to the wheels and rubbed his hands along the spokes he could reach. Soon after we turned off the main road onto the Haskells' road, Ty noticed a tall stem of white asters. He went to these and touched them. When I bent the stalk down so he could smell them, he leaned toward the flowers without a word. A few feet away were some purple asters. He saw these, touched them and smiled. Then he skipped down the lane, a child at last.

It is the healing force of nature with which Sarah Reynolds works through her organization, Animals as Intermediaries. She brings once-injured wild animals that cannot be restored to the wild to people institutionalized in hospitals and homes. On the floors of these places she builds environments of things she gathers in the meadows near her home in Concord, Massachusetts. And the people—imprisoned by illness, age, and fear—find themselves freed to speak, to care, to enter in. Finding life, they live. What Sarah presents is the world before language, before misunderstanding. It is the world before loss.

Three boys and I followed her on a short walk through the woods as she showed us, by touch and smell, the differences in the barks of trees, the shapes of leaves and needles, the low plants, the high, the places a squirrel had been. The two boys who were older copied all that Sarah did, touching everything as she touched it. Three-year-old Cory, meanwhile, wandered a little behind, engrossed in some adventure of his own until Sarah stopped at a patch of bright green moss and knelt to touch it. The two older boys touched it too, but quickly, perfunctorily. Cory sat down on the path next to the moss and ran his hand across it, pressed his hand down on it, into it, as if he would give himself entirely to this soft, yielding, gentle place in the forest. In the wonder on his face, I saw he had come to a magic place. Because I followed him, I had come there too.

A small girl, Shakia, brought me a story she had written on the bus from New York to Blueberry Cove. The story was printed in large letters on a single page. "It is fun to be on the bus," she wrote. "I am very happy." Giving her a notebook, I suggested she write a story every day so that, after a while, she would have a book. She beamed. I invited her for a walk to the high rock cliffs at the edge of the ocean. On top of the cliffs she sat bent over her notebook, so fully concentrated on her writing that I think she did not see the sea. Beyond her, the Atlantic rolled without stop into the cliffs, bright blue under a cloudless sky. High tide was past.

On the walk back, Shakia picked wildflowers along the road. As she picked them she showed me each new color and shape, then brought her bouquet to the lunch table. After lunch, she gave me her story to read. "We went on a long walk," she wrote. "I am very happy."

I walked her back to her cabin for rest period. Two babies were already asleep in the double bed. Shakia carefully placed her notebook on the shelf next to the bed, quietly took off her shoes, climbed over the baby at the edge and slipped beneath the covers between the two babies without waking either. I reached over to caress her face. Her dark skin was soft. It was like the softest silk. She smiled, then closed her eyes. I walked down to my tent and cried.

PART II

Disability and Disease

To Reconcile Oneself with the World

EDWARD STACHURA

*Translated from the Polish by Magda Zlotowska**

May 28, 1979

Monday. I slept fairly well. I was sweating a lot throughout the night, from exhaustion. Maybe it will go away. I watch my mother and the others, and I am learning from them how to delight in trifles, in small matters. Beautiful weather, air, well-baked bread and the like. People here speak normally about misfortunes. They take them to heart, but not for long.

In conversation they pass effortlessly from misfortunes to daily affairs. And it is healthy. Otherwise they would go mad. Just like me.

I used to know everything. Now it seems to me that I know nothing. But I do know "nothing." And I am this nothing. I am also very miserable and terribly lost. But it seems that I am slowly finding some morsel of peace again. Only with this will I be able to live. And with people.

In the hospital I wandered desperately back and forth. From break-

*This selection, from the last diaries of Polish poet and songwriter Edward Stachura, has been edited from the complete journal, published in Polish under the title, Pogodzić sie ze światem. This is the first translation into English.

fast till lunch, from lunch till supper. I could not find a place for myself. I could neither really walk nor sit, and when I stood it was with knees drawn in and with back bent and hunched as if waiting for the next blow. It was terrifying, that blow that I received in my back and in my head then, when I was standing motionless on the tracks. I heard the engineer blow the whistle twice, and I saw, after turning my head, how the locomotive drove straight at me—like a huge mountain. But I did not move. I stood rooted to the spot.

Now, I go with Mother to get water. On the way Mother picks some nettles for the chickens. Her hands are so toughened by toil that nettles don't sting her. To tell about this seems important to me since I have already interrupted the story of my second misfortune. It is cloudy outside. A little rain has fallen. Very little, but maybe it will rain some more. After two weeks of rainless scorching heat, the earth and plants really need it. Just as I am thirsty for I don't know what. Maybe for being without wishes, except the wish to possess that ability to live, which my mother and many other ordinary, truly simple people possess. At times I am seized with the panic that it is already too late for me to learn this in time. I console myself that it is not an inborn thing, but rather something that one acquires from day to day. Living at home with Mother from day to day, perhaps I will acquire it, or maybe it will appear in me by itself in some natural way.

Mother says it was the devil that possessed me and that after all I went through, I should go to confession. But I tell her that I am a good man, and that I always have been, maybe even abnormally good. My mother's faith in God and my longing are one and the same. One could call it trust. A little transistor radio plays on the table in the kitchen all day long, and pop music, song lyrics, commentaries of radio announcers and so forth do not irritate me any more. A human voice breathes out warmth, and I am all frozen inside, all covered with ice somehow, as though I had swallowed a huge icicle. Mother sits on a small couch in the kitchen and darns my shirt and pajamas, and I sit at the table and slowly and clumsily write one letter after another with this left hand of mine that remains. I manage to sit in one place without panic for longer periods of time. This is a definite change for the better, for the less terrible.

With Mother I feel safe. I feel safe with her.

How dexterous are human hands. They are able to do so much. Does one have to lose something in order to appreciate it? Waldek, the boy my mother hires for odd jobs she cannot handle herself—for example, chopping wood—nailed together a cage for the she-rabbit. I held scantlings and boards while he cut them. But of course he could also manage without me.

Two years ago, at the beginning of '77, I had painlessly lost Everything. Soon afterwards I received a new Everything. I was on the peak of a great mountain. It lasted for over two years. *Fabula Rasa (Or, The Question of Egoism)* and another text called *Here It Is* were written at that time. I say: "were written," and not "I wrote them," because it was as if not I, but someone else, had written them. That someone else called himself man-nobody. I was he and at the same time I wasn't. I find no other way to put it. At the end of March and in the first days of April, uncanny things started happening to me. During that time I was run over by a train, or perhaps only a locomotive, I still don't know. On the information sheet I saw in the hospital, it was written: hit by a locomotive, not by a train.

Again I lost Everything, but this time indescribably painfully. It has been like this for almost two months. It is as if I am deprived of senses, learning to taste everything that I see, hear, touch, everything that I eat, everything that I am writing here. I am also learning to dress myself with just one hand. The thumb, the only finger that remains from my right hand, proves to be so helpful. In many activities it almost replaces the whole hand of another man. The sun has come out. Mother went to hoe vegetables. Down by the pond I picked a basket of grass with clover for the rabbits. Before nine I will go to get milk from the Belters. The day is coming to an end. I have written a lot today. My left-handed writing is becoming more legible.

Wednesday, May 30

We were at the cemetery in Aleksandrow. It was an expedition as it is quite far. We had to walk through an entire village and the entire town. There was a lot of work because Mother tends many graves. We carried water from a faucet near the chapel and watered. Mother walked among graves as if in her own farmyard telling me who was who, when he died and how. She showed me where she would lie, together with her mother. She said all this normally. She is accustomed to it and to death.

I was a gentle rebel, the gentlest possible, but extreme. I went all the way. Was it too far? I wanted to take up all the misfortunes of man's world. And I went insane. But was it because of that? I don't know.

Now I am neither a rebel nor reconciled with the world. I would like to reconcile myself with the world, because my lot is unbearable. I cling to people, looking to them for relief and some kind of rescue. I don't know at what point I made a mistake, if I made one.

Monday, June 4

I am perhaps a little less panic-stricken today, maybe because I am taking medications now. But they stupefy too. In the hospital in Drewnica, where I was taking larger doses, I walked around drowsy all day long.

I did some exercises in the morning, just after getting up. I proceeded torpidly, especially with backward bends. My body is so sore. I was badly bruised. I feel it constantly in my back and chest. As for the right hand, fingers that were amputated are hurting me. Also the metacarpus that was amputated is hurting me. This phenomenon is given some name in medicine. Pandea, or maybe I am wrong.

What does not break you will strengthen you—people say. Let us hope! Let us hope! I would like to write something, some kind of book that would be titled *To Reconcile Oneself with the World*, with the left hand, from the heart. I speak as though I was not writing from the heart when I wrote with the right hand. Yet I always wrote from the heart.

My invincible fate, has it been broken? Or perhaps it has been bent, as though some powerful athlete took an iron bar and bent it however he liked on his knee, or simply in his hands. That which is hard, resistant, breaks. That which is soft, gentle, bends but does not break. What does not break you, will strengthen you. Let us hope! Let us hope!

Mother says it was an evil spirit that possessed me and was playing with me. "It was rushing, rushing at you, until you lost your mind. But slowly you will come back to yourself."

First I was crucified. I tell what I lived through, and I realize that it must sound mad, insane. But now I am lucid, and as one can see, I talk sense, not nonsense. Some of my companions in distress at the hospital in Drewnica would say a few phrases normally, and then suddenly interject a phrase betraying abnormality—for example, that I shouldn't worry about the hand because it would grow back.

Truly I don't know whether I can describe it all now, when it is so difficult for me to write and when it seems to me that I don't have a scrap of so-called literary talent.

On the first night of my incredible torments—from the succession of sleepless nights and days that lasted up till the accident on the tracks in Bednary—I was lying on the couch and started to hear different sounds: the howling of a dog, the movement of trees, somebody's breath, the crying of a small child, the banging of a window open and closed, rustling wafts of air, all this chilling the blood in my veins, precisely as people say.

Tuesday, June 5

Cloudless sky. People are waiting for rain. Because it hasn't rained for a long time. They say that the earth is dry and that rain would help, but they speak about it without rebellion, with some extraordinary reconciliation to their lot, which is bound to nature. The weather is good for haymaking, which is going on right now. Man-nobody, he was serene in all weather.

On the radio an actor is reading excerpts from the expedition of Jason and the Argonauts for the Golden Fleece. I listen to it as though it were a description of insanity lived through, and the Golden Fleece a liberation from it. I lived through terrifying uncanny things; I don't know if I will manage to describe it, but I know what I have lived through, psychically and physically. Also I don't think that it makes sense to describe in detail how I was crucified, how very real it was and how terribly it hurt; how very literally I died and was resurrected several times; how I was speaking in the voices of different people, how twice I became speechless, how very real it was, how I was divided into the left and right sides, how much it hurt, how I turned into half-woman and half-man, how very real it was, how I was talking to someone powerful, extremely powerful and intelligent, how I was begging him for muteness when I couldn't speak with him any more, even if it was euphoric; how I was begging him to kill me, how he was helping me to die, "manipulating" my breath, lips, nostrils, ear openings, and so on, it seems to me without end, but after all with an end, because now I am not living through it. All of that belongs to what psychiatrists call hallucinatory-delusive syndrome.

I am taking medications and I have a hard time concentrating, a hard time gathering thoughts. The medications' effect is stupefying and soporific. This is probably on purpose. Supposedly there is no good medication for this most mysterious of illnesses. Will I lift myself up? Won't it come back? I have to leave these questions without answers, as I do many others, as I do all questions that I pose. One man in Drewnica was telling me that every once in a while he returns to the hospital. "I am here already for the twenty-eighth time." Many were at home there, and it looked as if they were feeling fine. They were quiet, smiling, somehow they did not idle about so desperately as I did. Those who are serious cases are probably not unhappy. They are disconnected. They are beyond. It is worse for those like me, half-ill, half-healthy, aware of where they are, and witnessing all the abnormal behavior of others and themselves. Oh, how very unhappy they are. They walk and talk aloud to themselves: "Oh God, this hospital is hell. I will not endure it any longer here. They torture a man here with these shots." I said nothing, I only listened. I was walking back and forth as in a living cemetery, and I felt neither alive nor dead. I still feel this way. To be more precise, as alive, but without life. Or as dead, but without death. This state is inexpressibly terrible, and I wouldn't wish it on anyone, not even for a day.

June 7

This morning I did not feel the pain in my chest. In the evening Mother put a second pillow under my head and my back, which is probably why I don't feel the pain today. On the radio I hear that Jason has already gotten the Golden Fleece. He was helped by his companions and the sorceress Medea. Does that mean he has already passed through insanity and its monsters and freed himself, and will now be able to lead a normal life?

I brought drinking water from the Feleks, ate breakfast, took my medication and sat down to write. Days are long and to fill them with daily life is an ability which at present I do not possess and which I am learning from Mother and others by observing their activity in and around the house.

When I write, it isn't so bad, it could be worse. So let's write. I can write several hours a day. That's already a lot. Write about what? About the same. About myself. I have invented very few plots. It was unnecessary. Every man is a great mystery and it is enough to fathom oneself honestly, to describe one's own sensations and states and it is interesting.

Strawberries are in season and Mother has just picked some and brought me a plate of them sprinkled with sugar. On the 3rd of April I got a brain concussion on the tracks. Perhaps that is why I lost a lot of memory. I did not and still do not remember first and last names of people, names of towns, all kinds of data, pieces of information and the like. I write and speak in Polish as though after an interruption lasting dozens of years. I search for words in my head and I don't find them. I have also had difficulties in pronunciation. My tongue and lips were badly twisted. In the hospital in Drewnica I would stroll in the little forest and practice the alphabet aloud. From the beginning to the end, over and over again. Like a child. I'd look at trees, at objects, I would recollect names and speak them to myself aloud. Each time with more care. I also learned how to dress and undress and how to make the bed with just one hand. Truly, when one has two hands and then is left with just one, it is very, very frightening. All objects become aggressive. It seems that they are constructed against man, just to spite him. Yet it is normal that they are constructed for the two-handed, and further, for the right-handed, because etc. When I was studying at the University in Mexico, many students from the United States were left-handed. Almost all.

The copybook comes to an end, I've filled it with writing and I have to reach for a new one.

I write in a stream. Just as it comes.

When I published *Short Stories, Itself,* and *A Lot of Fire and So On,* I earned a lot of money. I gave it all away. I pushed it gently into the hands or pockets of old people I met in cafeterias where I used to eat. In this and other ways I gave away almost one hundred thousand zloty. I speak about it only in order to be able to raise the question: Was it normal?

When I had no more money, I started to give away objects and things which I had at home: shirts, pants, jackets, two beautiful Mexican ponchos, camera, radio, even my Brazilian guitar and other small things. Again I speak about it only in order to be able to ask the question: Was it normal?

Where does the normal end, where does the abnormal begin? That is the question. Where does bearable insanity end, and where does unbearable insanity begin?

I became a recluse in the midst of a great human community. Was it normal?

Scorching heat and no sign of rain. All around us, they say, it rains, but not here.

Rain passes over this place. I was in the field, picked a basket of dandelions. Now I am going to get milk, because already, or rather, finally, evening has come. Goodnight.

The Farme of Man

JOHN DONNE

Sit morbi fomes tibi cura;
The Physitians consider the root and occasion, the embers, and
coales, and fuell of the disease, and seek to purge or correct that.

How ruinous a farme hath man taken, in taking himselfe! How ready
is the house every day to fall downe, and how is all the ground over-
spread with weeds, all the body with diseases! where not onely every
turfe, but every stone, beares weeds; not onely every muscle of the
flesh, but every bone of the body, hath some infirmitie; every little
flint upon the face of this soile, hath some infectious weede, every
tooth in our head, such a paine as a constant man is afraid of, and yet
ashamed of that feare, of that sense of the paine. How deare, and how
often a rent doth Man pay for this farme! hee paies twice a day, in
double meales, and how little time he hath to raise his rent! How
many holy daies to call him from his labour! Every day is halfe-holy
day, halfe spent in sleepe. What reparations, and subsidies, and con-
tributions he is put to, besides his rent! What medicines, besides his
diet! and what Inmates he is faine to take in, besides his owne fami-
lie, what infectious diseases, from other men! Adam might have had
Paradise for dressing and keeping it; and then his rent was not

73

improved to such a labour, as would have made his brow sweat; and yet he gave it over; how farre greater a rent doe wee pay for this farme, this body, who pay our selves, who pay the farme it selfe, and cannot live upon it! Neither is our labour at an end, when wee have cut downe some weed, as soone as it sprung up, corrected some violent and dangerous accident of a disease, which would have destroied speedily; nor when wee have pulled up that weed, from the very root, recovered entirely and soundly, from that particular disease; but the whole ground is of an ill nature, the whole soile ill disposed; there are inclinations, there is a propensenesse to diseases in the body, out of which without any other disorder, diseases will grow, and so wee are put to a continuall labour upon this farme, to a continuall studie of the whole complexion and constitution of our body. In the distempers and diseases of soiles, sourenesse, drinesse, weeping, any kind of barrennesse, the remedy and the physicke, is, for a great part, sometimes in themselves; sometime[s] the very situation releeves them; the hanger of a hill, will purge and vent his owne malignant moisture; and the burning of the upper turfe of some ground (as health from cauterizing) puts a new and a vigorous youth into that soile, and there rises a kinde of Phoenix out of the ashes, a fruitfulnesse out of that which was barren before, and by that, which is the barrennest of all, ashes. And where the ground cannot give it selfe Physicke, yet it receives Physicke from other grounds, from other soiles, which are not the worse, for having contributed that helpe to them, from Marle in other hils, or from slimie sand in other shoares: grounds helpe themselves, or hurt not other grounds, from whence they receive helpe. But I have taken a farme at this hard rent, and upon those heavie covenants, that it can afford it self no helpe; (no part of my body, if it were cut off, would cure another part; in some cases it might preserve a sound part, but in no case recover an infected) and, if my body may have any Physicke, any Medicine from another body, one Man from the flesh of another Man (as by Mummy, or any such composition,) it must bee from a man that is dead, and not, as in other soiles, which are never the worse for contributing their Marle, or their fat slime to my ground. There is nothing in the same man, to helpe man, nothing in mankind to helpe one another (in this sort, by way of Physicke) but that hee who ministers the helpe, is in as ill case, as he that receives it would have beene, if he had not had it; for hee from whose body the Physicke comes, is dead. When therefore I tooke this farme, undertooke this body, I undertooke to draine, not a marish, but a moat, where there was, not water mingled to offend, but all was water; I undertooke to perfume dung, where no one part, but all was equally unsavory; I undertooke to make such a thing wholsome, as was not poison by any manifest quality, intense heat, or cold, but poison in the whole substance, and in the specifique forme of it. To cure the sharpe accidents of diseases, is a great worke; to cure the disease it selfe is a greater; but to cure the body, the root, the occasion of diseases, is a worke reserved for the great Phisitian, which he doth never any other way, but by glorifying these bodies in the next world.

Even at Night, the Sun Is There

GRAY HENRY

A few years ago I was living in an English village outside Cambridge while researching my doctorate and working with the Islamic Texts Society, an academic organization which publishes important works from the Islamic heritage after having had them translated into English.

One evening as I reached to switch off the bedside lamp, I noticed my arm would not stretch out to do so. In fact, I found I was not able to pull the blankets up about me except by using my teeth; neither arm seemed to function. When I tried to take a deep breath it seemed as though my lungs were incapable of expansion. At the approach of a cough or sneeze, I held my arms closely around my chest for fear the sudden and painful enlargement of my breast would rip me apart. When I arose the next morning, the only way to get out of bed was to hang my knees over the edge and slide off since my upper torso had become powerless. I couldn't even raise my arms to brush my hair. Turning the bathroom faucet was an excruciating affair. By holding the bottom of the steering wheel in my finger tips, I was able to drive to the village clinic. The doctor concluded I had some type of virus for which there was no treatment other than time.

A day or so later, my husband and I were to fly to Boston for the annual congress of the Middle East Studies Association. I viewed my affliction as an inconvenience which would ultimately pass and decided to ignore my condition. I noticed, however, that on the day we were to leave England I began to have trouble walking, and getting upstairs was extremely difficult. By the time we reached the hotel room in Boston, more and more of my system seemed to be shutting down. I could no longer write or hold a tea cup, bite anything as formidable as an apple, dress myself, or even get out of a chair unless assisted. Everything ached. I could not move my head in the direction of the people I was speaking to—I looked straight ahead, perhaps seeing them from the corner of my eye.

Friends gave all kinds of advice that I simply shrugged off. The worst part was lying in bed at night. It was impossible to roll on to either side, and my whole body felt on fire with pain. It was terrible to have to lie flat, unable to make any shift whatsoever all night long. I thought to myself, "If only I could scratch my cheek when it itched, if only my eyes were not dry but cool, if only I could swallow without it feeling like a ping-pong-sized ball of pain, if only I could reach for a glass of water when thirsty during the long night."

As we traveled on for work in New York, I continued to make light of my infirmity and to ignore suggestions that I seek help. On the plane, however, when it was necessary to ask the stewardess to tear open the paper sugar packet, I suddenly realized—"I can't even tear a piece of paper!" I requested that a wheelchair await me in New York and that I be transferred to a flight home to my parents in Louisville, Kentucky. Since my husband was obliged to stay in New York, a kind soldier returning to Fort Knox helped me during that leg of the trip. I felt like a wounded fox that wanted nothing more than to return to, and curl up alone in, the nest of its childhood. My father met me, and the next day took me for every test imaginable. Nothing was conclusively established—was this rheumatoid arthritis, or lupus? I was brought to my parents' house and at last put in my childhood bed with a supply of painkillers, which I was not inclined to take. I found I could tolerate great pain, since I wanted to observe the situation and know where I stood. I started seeing my body as an object separate from me and my mind, which witnessed its ever-declining condition. When my legs finally "went," with knees swollen like grapefruits and feet incapable of bearing me up, I mused with a kind of detached interest, "Oh, there go the legs!" The body seemed to be mine, but it was not *me*.[1] Later that night *it* happened. As I lay gazing out my bedroom door and noticed the carpet in the quiet hall, I thought, "Thank God I'm not in a hospital and the hall is not linoleum and that I am not subjected to the clatter of ice machines and the chatter of nurses. I know I'm in trouble and I do need help, but *that* would be too great a cost for my soul."

A few moments later I became aware that I seemed to be solidifying, my body had stiffened and seemed to be very much like a log—I was totally paralyzed. Then, I seemed to separate from my body and lift a distance above it. I glanced back and saw my head on the pillow and thought, "This is remarkable—I've read about this kind of thing...*I* am thinking and my brain is down there in my head! I must be *dead*." I considered what to do. At the moment of death in Islam, the dying person repeats the *shahada* "There is no divinity except God."

As I thought the phrase, "*La ilaha ilallah,*" I noticed that I seemed to be pulled back towards my heart—as if by a thread of light. But then there I was—quite all right, but utterly rigid and still. The light of the moon comforted me as it passed through the leafless November branches making patterns on the blankets. I thought, "Even at night, the Sun is there. Even in darkness and death, the Light is present." The season seemed to parallel my state.

I then began to imagine my future. I have friends who are paralyzed who have always been placed along the sidelines for various events. Had I now joined them? Was I now out of the normal life of others? I began to see myself like a hunchback or a dwarf. I had always been known for my inexhaustible energy and activities. I could always, somehow, get to my feet and do one more thing. This was now over. I would no longer be able to *do* anything. I thought of people in this world who have impressed me most—the Mother Teresas of our world. I realized that what was exemplary in these people was not what they *did*, but what they *were*; the state of *being* which determined their movement was what actually inspired others. And so I set upon a plan of inward action: The best thing I could do for others would be to sanctify my soul, to let my state of being become radiant. Having concluded this, I felt things were in order.

In the morning I was found, fixed in place; I was given eggnog—chewing was over. My husband came from New York and I recall marvelling when I observed him. He could, without considering the matter in depth, shift his position in a chair, scratch his forehead, or lean over to pick up a dropped pencil—all painlessly! Imagine—reflex action! Occasionally if I really wanted to move, for example, my fingers, I would think to myself, "All right, now, I-am-going-to-try-to-move-my-fingers," and I would concentrate my entire attention on the task. With *incredible* pain and focus, I could at most shift a few millimeters. It struck me profoundly that when someone is able to move in this world without pain—that is, in health—that he *resides in paradise on earth* without ever being aware of it. Everything after that is *extra*.

Ultimately, it was decided that I should be given a week's course of cortisone so I could return to my children and the British specialist who might be able to figure out what I had. The cortisone was miraculous and frightening—I could actually walk and pick up things—yet I knew that I couldn't.

On the return to Cambridge, it was decided that I should be removed overnight from the cortisone. I then discovered what withdrawal symptoms are—a level of pain that seems to consume one alive with fire. But the pain was nothing compared to the frightening mental confusion I experienced: I could not grasp proper thinking, or even normal reality. What I needed was not only a doctor, but a kind of scholar/saint who could describe to me the hierarchy of meaning so that I would not be so painfully lost. I suppose true doctors are a combination of all three. The Islamic physician/philosopher was called a *hakim* (a word which refers to wisdom). I grasped some rosaries and clung to them like lifelines thrown to a drowning man, and I made it to the light of dawn on the invocation of God's Name, my sanity intact.

The English specialist could not make a conclusive diagnosis. Our Vietnamese acupuncturist suggested toxins had built up in the entire muscle system and prescribed massage during steam baths to release them. It sounded definitely worth doing. At the same time, I had come to that point that the very ill come to, where, though they take advice with gratitude, inside of them something has dimmed and they no longer wish to make any effort. Pleasantly, I had reached a great calm within. Each day I was brought downstairs where I directed the preparation of meals and worried the children, who saw I could no longer sew on a button or sign a check. I was resigned to never moving again. I had never experienced such peace. It was touching that people prayed for me and it was lovely that so many asked after my condition. I felt like an upright pole stuck in the middle of a moving stream.

In the spring, my husband had work in Arabia and suggested that as he would be travelling by private plane I could as easily sit in a dry climate as I could in cold, damp Cambridge. I agreed to go. On my arrival a dear friend managed to get me to Mecca. She thought that prayers in the mosque there would help. But when I found myself before the Kaa'ba, I felt it would be wrong to pray for my affliction to be lifted, as its good had come to outweigh its bad, in terms of my heart and soul.

A few days later I was asked to give a talk in Jeddah. I declined, explaining that I was unable to research and prepare a topic properly. Friends said they would be delighted to do this, if I could come up with a subject. I answered, "All right, why does *THIS* happen to someone, in the view of Islam?" The passages they wrote down and translated to English from both the Koran and *hadith*, the sayings and recorded deeds of the Prophet Muhammad—all seemed to say the *same* thing. In Islam, illness is understood to be a great blessing because it is an opportunity, if borne with patience free of complaint, to purify oneself of past sins—to burn away wrong thoughts and deeds.

As I delivered my talk, it began to dawn upon me why Muslims always reply with *Al hamdulilah* (the same as *Alleluia*) whenever anyone inquires as to their health. I had always wondered why one could ask someone who suffered from an obviously terrible physical or emotional pain or loss, "How *are* you," and all one could get out of him was, "All praise belongs to God." I kept wanting them to talk about their pain with me, to share their suffering, and I wondered why they would not. *Suddenly I realized that they were praising God for their state of being.* The suffering they endured, no matter how great or small, was an opportunity to be purified, which is the very aim of human existence. In an instant, my own illness was seen in a new light. I no longer patiently tolerated it—*I loved it, I flowed with it.* I saw how blessed I was to have been given, not something small, but something as total as paralysis.

As I loved my illness, my fingers suddenly began to regain movement. Bit by bit the movement in my hands returned, until at last in late spring, I was restored. What had been the most painful and difficult time in my life turned out to be the best thing that ever happened to me. I had gained a deepened perspective, a sense of proportion and freedom. God had blessed me with near total dependence on others, a symbol reminding me of my utter dependency on Him. And even when I had not been able to move one inch, I was able to be in touch with His Divine Presence.

O God, to Thee belongs praise for the good health of my body which lets me move about, and to Thee belongs praise, for the ailments which Thou causes to arise in my flesh!

For I know not, my God, which of the two states deserves more my thanking Thee and which of the two times is more worthy for my praise of Thee:

the time of health,
within which Thou makest me delight in the agreeable things of Thy provision, through which Thou givest me the joy to seek the means to Thy good pleasure and bounty, and by which Thou strengthenest me for the acts of obedience which Thou hast given me to accomplish;

or the time of illness
through which Thou puttest me to the test and bestowest upon me

81

favors: lightening of the offenses that weigh down my back, purification of the evil deeds into which I have plunged, incitement to reach for repentance, reminder of the erasure of misdeeds through ancient favor; and, through all that, what the two writers[2] write for me.

—Imam Zayn al Abidin Ali ibn al Husayn,
Al Sahifat Al Kamilat Al Sajjadiyya
(*William Chittick, tr.*)

(The illness described above was later diagnosed as Guillain-Barré Syndrome.)

NOTES
1. "Islamic physicians saw the body of man as but an extension of his soul and closely related to both the spirit and the soul...They envisaged the subject of medicine, namely man, to be related both inwardly through the soul and the spirit, and 'outwardly' through the grades of the macrocosmic hierarchy to the principle of cosmic manifestation itself.... whatever may have been the historical origins of Islamic Medicine, its principles cannot be understood save in the light of Islamic metaphysical and cosmological sciences." S.H. Nasr, "Theory of Islamic Medicine," in *Islamic Science* (London: World of Islam Festival Publishing Co. Ltd., 1976), p. 159.
2. According to Islamic belief there is an angel on either shoulder who records one's good and bad deeds.

Writing as a Healing Process

Anatole Broyard

Storytelling seems to be a natural reaction to illness. People bleed stories, and I've become a blood bank of them.

The patient has to start by treating his illness not as a disaster, an occasion for depression or panic, but as a narrative, a story. Stories are antibodies against illness and pain. When various doctors shoved scopes up my urethral canal, I found that it helped a lot when they gave me a narrative of what they were doing. Their talking translated or humanized the procedure. It prepared, strengthened, and somehow consoled me. Anything is better than an awful silent suffering.

I sometimes think that silence can kill you, like that terrible scene at the end of Kafka's *The Trial* when Joseph K. dies speechlessly, "like a dog." In "The Metamorphosis," a story that is now lodged in everybody's unconscious, Gregor Samsa dies like an insect. To die is to be no longer human, to be dehumanized—and I think that language, speech, stories, or narratives are the most effective ways to keep our humanity alive. To remain silent is literally to close down the shop of one's humanity.

One of my friends had lung cancer, and during an exploratory operation he suffered a stroke that left him speechless. For a month he lay in his hospital bed trying to talk to me and his other friends with his eyes. He was too depressed or too traumatized to write on a pad. He died not of cancer exactly, but of pneumonia, as if his lungs had filled with trapped speech and he had drowned in it.

Just as a novelist turns his anxiety into a story in order to be able to control it to a degree, so a sick person can make a story, a narrative, out of his illness as a way of trying to detoxify it. In the beginning I invented mininarratives. Metaphor was one of my symptoms. I saw my illness as a visit to a disturbed country, rather like contemporary China. I imagined it as a love affair with a demented woman who demanded things I had never done before. I thought of it as a lecture I was about to give to an immense audience on a subject that had not been specified. Having cancer was like moving from a cozy old Dickensian house crammed with antiques, deep sofas, snug corners, and fireplaces to a brand-new one that was all windows, skylights, and tubular furniture.

Making narratives like this rescues me from the unknown, from what Ernest Becker called "the panic inherent in creation" or "the suction of infinity." If I were to demystify or deconstruct my cancer, I might find that there is no absolute diagnosis, no single agreed-upon text, but only the interpretation each doctor and each patient makes. Thinking about difficult situations is what writers do best. Poetry, for example, might be defined as language writing itself out of a difficult situation.

Writing is a counterpoint to my illness. It forces the cancer to go through my character before it can get to me. In *Intensive Care*, Mary-Lou Weisman tells us that just before her fifteen-year old son died of muscular dystrophy, he asked his father to arrange him in an "impudent position" in the hospital bed. I'd like my writing to be impudent. While Norman Cousins looks for healing laughter in low comedy, I'd rather try to find it in wit. The threat of dying ought to make people witty, since they are already concentrated. Oddly enough, death fits Freud's economic definition of wit: He says that we set aside a certain amount of energy to hear out a joke that threatens to go on and on like life, and then suddenly the punch line cuts across it, freeing all that energy for a rush of pleasure.

Norman Cousins and Bernie Siegel are correct in saying that a sick person needs other strategies besides medical ones to help him cope with his illness, and I think it might be useful to describe some of the strategies that have occurred to me. After all, a critic is a kind of doctor of strategies. For example, I saw on television an Afro-Cuban band playing in the streets of Spanish Harlem. It was a very good band, and before long a man stepped out of the crowd and began dancing. He was very good, too, even though he had only one leg and was dancing on crutches. He danced on those crutches as other people dance on ice skates, and I think that there's probably a "dance" for every condition. As Kenneth Burke, one of our best literary critics, said, the symbolic act is the dancing of an attitude.

As a preparation for writing, as a first step toward evolving a strategy for my illness, I've begun to take tap-dancing lessons, something I've always wanted to do. One of my favorite examples of a patient's strategy comes from a man I know who also has prostate cancer. Instead of imagining his good cells attacking his bad cells, he goes to Europe from time to time and imposes Continental images on his bad cells. He reminds me that in an earlier, more holistic age, doctors used to advise sick people to go abroad for their health.

The illness genre ought to have a literary critic—in addition to or in reply to Susan Sontag—to talk about the therapeutic value of style, for it seems to me that every seriously ill person needs to develop a style for his illness. I think that only by insisting on your style can you keep from falling out of love with yourself as the illness attempts to diminish or disfigure you. Sometimes your vanity is the only thing that's keeping you alive, and your style is the instrument of your vanity. It may not be dying we fear so much, but the diminished self.

I would also like a doctor who *enjoyed* me. I want to be a good story for him, to give him some of my art in exchange for his. If a patient expects a doctor to be interested in him, he ought to try to *be* interesting. When he shows nothing but a greediness for care, nothing but the coarser forms of anxiety, it's only natural for the doctor to feel an aversion. There is an etiquette to being sick. I never act sick with my doctor. As I've said, I have been accelerated by my illness, and when my doctor comes in, I juggle him. I toss him about. I throw him from hand to hand, and he hardly knows what to do with me. I never act sick. A puling person is not appealing.

I have a wistful desire for our relationship to be beautiful in some way that I can't quite identify. A famous Surrealist dictum says that "Beauty is the chance meeting, on an operating table, of a sewing machine and an umbrella." Perhaps we could be beautiful like that. Just as he orders blood tests and bone scans of my body, I'd like my doctor to scan *me*, to grope for my spirit as well as my prostate. Without some such recognition, I am nothing but my illness.

While he inevitably feels superior to me because he is the doctor and I am the patient, I'd like him to know that I feel superior to him, too, that he is my patient also and I have my diagnosis of him. There should be a place where our respective superiorities could meet and frolic together. Finally, I would be happier with a witty doctor who could appreciate the comedy as well as the tragedy of my illness, its quirks and eccentricities, the final jokes of a personality that has nothing further to lose.

I find an irresistible desire to make jokes. When you're lying in the hospital with a catheter and IV in your arm, you have two choices, self-pity or irony. If the doctor doesn't get your ironies, who else is there around?

Transforming Our Suffering

THICH NHAT HANH

Over the last few years, Vietnamese Zen Master Thich Nhat Hanh has led retreats in the U.S. for veterans of the Vietnam War. One of the themes on which he focuses is the transformation of suffering as an essential part of healing for those who have been active participants in and victims of war. As a result of this work, at least one Vietnam veteran is now leading workshops and speaking to other veterans on healing the wounds of war.

Our society is full of violence, hatred, and fear, and we are influenced by that. Young people growing up today receive many seeds of unhappiness. Why are we so violent? Why is there so much fear and hatred in us? It is because there is so much violence, hatred, and fear in society, in our collective consciousness. A society like ours will always produce police like the ones who beat up Rodney King. If we fire policemen or lock them in prison, we will not solve the problem, because the roots of the problem are in society. A policeman knows he has to take care of himself, because he can be killed by anyone on the street. A poor person on a motorcycle can kill him; a rich person in a Mercedes can kill him.

Police must cultivate fear every day. They know that if they are not quicker than the other, they may be killed. Motivated by this fear, they may shoot someone by mistake. One week before the beating of Rodney King, a policewoman was shot in the face by another driver when she asked to see his driver's license. Other police in the area went to her funeral filled with hatred and fear.

When 500,000 American soldiers went to the Persian Gulf, they too were forced to cultivate violence and fear. Their mothers, wives, husbands, and children wanted them to return home alive. They, too, wanted to come home alive, so they had to practice killing. A regular human being cannot kill another human being. To be able to kill, you have to become a beast. I happened to see five seconds of a newscast on French television showing the training of American soldiers in Saudi Arabia. They were jumping and shouting in order to become something less than themselves, so they would be in the state of mind to plunge bayonets into other human beings. The soldiers had to practice this every day. They had to visualize Saddam Hussein to generate enough hatred in themselves to be able to kill Iraqi soldiers. They practiced violence, fear, and hatred for six or seven months, every day and at night in their dreams.

A doctor who went with them told me that when a soldier begins to pull the trigger on his automatic weapon, he is too afraid to stop. He thinks if he stops firing he will be fired upon and killed. He listens only to his fear and continues to shoot until he runs out of bullets. A soldier in that situation cannot listen to anything but his fear, not even to the orders of his superior. When you are in that situation every day, you water the seeds of fear, hatred, and violence in yourself. What will become of your consciousness after six months of practicing like that?

The Buddha said, "This is, because that is. This is not, because that is not. This is like this, because that is like that." Society is like this, that is why the way you handle a conflict must be like this. Society is only a manifestation of our collective consciousness, and our collective consciousness has a lot of fear, violence, and hatred in it. If we were to photograph the consciousness of the soldier and compare it with a photograph of the collective consciousness of the nation, we would see that they are both the same.

The healing of ourselves is the healing of the whole nation. The practice of mindfulness is crucial. We need to be mindful of the true nature of war and we need to share the fruits of our insight with our whole society. War is a reflection of our collective consciousness. The war was not just in Iraq, or Vietnam. The war is present every day in our society. We have so much violence, hatred, and fear, and it is expressed in our magazines, television, films, and advertisements. There is so much deep suffering, deep malaise in people. Look at the way people consume drugs as a way to forget. These are the seeds of war that we have to acknowledge if we want to transform them. We have to do it together, looking deeply into the nature of war in our collective consciousness. War is in our souls.

In the teaching of Buddhism, shame, guilt, or regret can be beneficial. When you realize that what you do causes damage, and if you make the vow not to do it again, that feeling of regret can be a wholesome and beneficial mental attribute. But if that guilt, shame or regret persists too long and becomes a guilt complex, it becomes unwholesome and blocks the way of joy and peace. The only way to liberate yourself from that blockage is to look deeply into the nature of that guilt and self-hatred. When we look into the nature of the seeds of our suffering, we can see our ancestors, our parents, and the violence and lack of understanding in our society and in ourselves.

When the sun rises in the sky, it projects its light on the vegetation. That is all the sun needs to do to help. The green color that is seen in the vegetation is the work of the sun. The sun does the work of transformation. Imagine a flower in the early morning—a tulip or a lotus. The sun shines on the flower. It is not satisfied with going around the flower. It makes every effort to penetrate it. The sunshine penetrates the flower, either in the form of particles or in the form of waves. The flower may still resist and stay closed for a while. But if the sun persists in shining for two or three hours, a transformation will occur. The flower will have to open itself to show its heart to the sun.

Our anger is a kind of flower, and our mindfulness is the sun continuing to shine upon it. Do not be impatient. The very first moment you shine your awareness on it, there is already some transformation within your anger.

When we boil potatoes, we put the potatoes into a pot of cold water on the fire, and we put a cover on it. The fire is the presence of mindfulness. The potatoes will not be cooked in a few seconds. We have to keep the fire going. We have to nourish the fire. We do this with the power of our concentration.

When we practice mindfulness, we breathe consciously. We do not watch television or disperse our energies in a conversation, because these things disperse the heat. Concentration is needed to make mindfulness strong. We put the cover on the pot and the water will begin to warm up right away. If we continue to practice, the potatoes will get cooked and will become quite delicious. Anger is like that; when it is raw, it's awful, but when you cook it, it becomes trans-formed into understanding and acceptance.

Transformation is the word. We can do the work of transformation only in the present moment. The Buddha said that the ocean of suf-fering is immense, but when you concentrate on transforming it, you will see the shore and the land right away. It is possible to transform our heart, to transform our compost and offer the world a rose, in the present moment. Not much time is needed. The rose can be born right away, the moment you vow to go in the direction of peace and service.

Therefore, we should not dwell only in our suffering. If we look deeply into it, we will know what to do and what not to do to trans-form our heart and change our present situation. My brothers and sis-ters and their babies who died during the war in Vietnam have now been reborn into flowers. We have to harvest these flowers. When we learn from our own suffering, then all the flowers will be smiling at us.

Germs

LEWIS THOMAS

Watching television, you'd think we lived at bay, in total jeopardy, surrounded on all sides by human-seeking germs, shielded against infection and death only by a chemical technology that enables us to keep killing them off. We are instructed to spray disinfectants everywhere, into the air of our bedrooms and kitchens and with special energy into our bathrooms, since it is our very own germs that seem the worst kind. We explode clouds of aerosol, mixed for good luck with deodorants, into our noses, mouths, underarms, privileged crannies—even into the intimate insides of our telephones. We apply potent antibiotics to minor scratches and seal them with plastic. Plastic is the new protector; we wrap the already plastic tumblers of hotels in more plastic, and seal the toilet seats like state secrets after irradiating them with ultraviolet light. We live in a world where the microbes are always trying to get at us, to tear us cell from cell, and we only stay alive and whole through diligence and fear.

We still think of human disease as the work of an organized, modernized kind of demonology, in which the bacteria are the most visible and centrally placed of our adversaries. We assume that they must somehow relish what they do. They come after us for profit, and there are so many of them that disease seems inevitable, a natural part of

91

the human condition; if we succeed in eliminating one kind of disease there will always be a new one at hand, waiting to take its place.

These are paranoid delusions on a societal scale, explainable in part by our need for enemies, and in part by our memory of what things used to be like. Until a few decades ago, bacteria were a genuine household threat, and although most of us survived them, we were always aware of the nearness of death. We moved, with our families, in and out of death. We had lobar pneumonia, meningococcal meningitis, streptococcal infections, diphtheria, endocarditis, enteric fevers, various septicemias, syphilis, and, always, everywhere, tuberculosis. Most of these have now left most of us, thanks to antibiotics, plumbing, civilization, and money, but we remember.

In real life, however, even in our worst circumstances we have always been a relatively minor interest of the vast microbial world. Pathogenicity is not the rule. Indeed, it occurs so infrequently and involves such a relatively small number of species, considering the huge population of bacteria on the Earth, that it has a freakish aspect. Disease usually results from inconclusive negotiations for symbiosis, an overstepping of the line by one side or the other, a biologic misinterpretation of borders.

Some bacteria are only harmful to us when they make exotoxins, and they only do this when they are, in a sense, diseased themselves. The toxins of diphtheria bacilli and streptococci are produced when the organisms have been infected by bacteriophage; it is the virus that provides the code for toxin. Uninfected bacteria are uninformed. When we catch diphtheria it is a virus infection, but not of us. Our involvement is not that of an adversary in a straightforward game, but more like blundering into someone else's accident.

I can think of a few microorganisms, possibly the tubercle bacillus, the syphilis spirochete, the malarial parasite, and a few others, that have a selective advantage in their ability to infect human beings, but there is nothing to be gained, in an evolutionary sense, by the capacity to cause illness or death. Pathogenicity may be something of a disadvantage for most microbes, carrying lethal risks more frightening to them than to us. The man who catches a meningococcus is in considerably less danger for his life, even without chemotherapy, than meningococci with the bad luck to catch a man. Most meningococci have the sense to stay out on the surface, in the rhinopharynx. During epidemics this is where they are to be found in the majority of the host population, and it generally goes well. It is only in the unaccountable minority, the "cases," that the line is crossed, and then there is the devil to pay on both sides, but most of all for the meningococci.

Staphylococci live all over us, and seem to have adapted to conditions in our skin that are uncongenial to most other bacteria. When you count them up, and us, it is remarkable how little trouble we have with the relation. Only a few of us are plagued by boils, and we can blame a large part of the destruction of tissues on the zeal of our own leukocytes. Hemolytic streptococci are among our closest intimates, even to the extent of sharing antigens with the membranes of our muscle cells; it is our reaction to their presence, in the form of rheumatic fever, that gets us into trouble. We can carry brucella for long periods in the cells of our reticuloendothelial system without any awareness of their existence; then cyclically, for reasons not understood but probably related to immunologic reactions on our part, we sense them, and the reaction of sensing is the clinical disease.

Most bacteria are totally preoccupied with browsing, altering the configurations of organic molecules so that they become usable for the energy needs of other forms of life. They are, by and large, indispensable to each other, living in interdependent communities in the soil or sea. Some have become symbionts in more specialized, local relations, living as working parts in the tissues of higher organisms. The root nodules of legumes would have neither form nor function without the masses of rhizobial bacteria swarming into root hairs, incorporating themselves with such intimacy that only an electron microscope can detect which membranes are bacterial and which plant. Insects have colonies of bacteria, the mycetocytes, living in them like little glands, doing heaven knows what but being essential. The microfloras of animal intestinal tracts are part of the nutritional system. And then, of course, there are the mitochondria and chloroplasts, permanent residents in everything.

The microorganisms that seem to have it in for us in the worst way—the ones that really appear to wish us ill—turn out on close examination to be rather more like bystanders, strays, strangers in from the cold. They will invade and replicate if given the chance, and some of them will get into our deepest tissues and set forth in the blood, but it is our response to their presence that makes the disease. Our arsenals for fighting off bacteria are so powerful, and involve so many different defense mechanisms, that we are in more danger from them than from the invaders. We live in the midst of explosive devices; we are mined.

It is the information carried by the bacteria that we cannot abide.

The gram-negative bacteria are the best examples of this. They display lipopolysaccharide endotoxin in their walls, and these macro-molecules are read by our tissues as the very worst of bad news. When we sense lipopolysaccharide, we are likely to turn on every defense at our disposal; we will bomb, defoliate, blockade, seal off, and destroy all the tissues in the area. Leukocytes become more actively phagocyt-ic, release lysosomal enzymes, turn sticky, and aggregate together in dense masses, occluding capillaries and shutting off the blood supply. Complement is switched on at the right point in its sequence to release chemotactic signals, calling in leukocytes from everywhere. Vessels become hyperreactive to epinephrine so that physiologic con-centrations suddenly possess necrotizing properties. Pyrogen is released from leukocytes, adding fever to hemorrhage, necrosis, and shock. It is a shambles.

All of this seems unnecessary, panic-driven. There is nothing intrinsically poisonous about endotoxin, but it must look awful, or feel awful, when sensed by cells. Cells believe that it signifies the presence of gram-negative bacteria, and they will stop at nothing to avoid this threat.

I used to think that only the most highly developed, civilized ani-mals could be fooled in this way, but it is not so. The horseshoe crab is a primitive fossil of a beast, ancient and uncitified, but he is just as vulnerable to disorganization by endotoxin as a rabbit or a man. It has been shown that an injection of a very small dose into the body cavi-ty will cause the aggregation of hemocytes in ponderous, immovable masses that block the vascular channels, and a gelatinous clot brings the circulation to a standstill. It is now known that a limulus clotting system, perhaps ancestral to ours, is centrally involved in the reaction. Extracts of the hemocytes can be made to jell by adding extremely small amounts of endotoxin. The self-disintegration of the whole animal that follows a systemic injection can be interpreted as a well-intentioned but lethal error. The mechanism is itself quite a good one, when used with precision and restraint, admirably designed for coping with intrusion by a single bacterium: the hemocyte would be attracted to the site, extrude the coagulable protein, the microorganism would be entrapped and immobilized, and the thing would be finished. It is when confronted by the overwhelming signal of free modules of endotoxin, evoking memories of vibrios in great numbers, that the limulus flies into panic, launches all his defenses at once, and destroys himself.

It is, basically, a response to propaganda, something like the panic-producing pheromones that slave-taking ants release to disorganize the colonies of their prey.

I think it likely that many of our diseases work in this way. Sometimes the mechanisms used for overkill are immunologic, but often, as in the limulus model, they are more primitive kinds of memory. We tear ourselves to pieces because of symbols, and we are more vulnerable to this than to any host of predators. We are, in effect, at the mercy of our own Pentagons, most of the time.

An Encounter

MARVIN BARRETT

*Come ye blessed of my Father, inherit the kingdom prepared for
you from the foundation of the world;*
*For I was an hungred, and ye gave me meat: I was thirsty, and ye
gave me drink: I was a stranger, and ye took me in:*
*Naked, and ye clothed me; I was sick and ye visited me; I was in
prison, and ye came unto me.*
*Then shall the righteous answer him, saying, Lord, when saw we
thee an hungred, and fed thee? or thirsty, and gave thee drink?*
*When saw we thee a stranger, and took thee in? or naked and
clothed thee?*
Or when saw we thee sick, or in prison, and came unto thee?
*And the King shall answer and say unto them, Verily I say unto
you, Inasmuch as ye have done it unto one of the least of these my
brethren, ye have done it unto me.*

—Matthew 25: 34-40

This afternoon waiting for the crosstown bus at 79th and Third
Avenue, leaning wearily against the shelter support—a long wait—I
saw Christ.

It was a very simple sharp vision. Coming toward me across the intersection an old man in a grey raincoat and a stitched narrow-brimmed cloth hat lost his footing, slipped and fell to the pavement. Not close enough so that my instant reflex was to reach out and pick him up—not so close as the man who was bending over and touching him, nor as the girl in green who had made a gesture in his direction and after a moment, looking anxiously at the light that was about to change, kept on walking. For me, there was a gap, a moment of reticence, of unworthiness or *pudeur*, and then I ran out. Between us, the other man and I got the old man to his feet. For a minute he seemed limp—at least resistant to being helped—and I observed to myself that his dead weight, which I was struggling to get upright, certainly represented a great deal more than the fifteen pounds allowed me by my cardiologist.

Somehow the two of us steered him to the curb. The street was strangely silent. There was no honking, no expression of impatience from cabbies or truck drivers nor people in sports cars leaning out of their windows, urging us to get out of the way.

Once we got him to the curb and standing shakily, traffic resumed. The other helper, assuring himself that the old man was ambulatory and that I was willing to take over, moved on. So I was left with a trembling grey-haired man with two brutally scraped and bleeding hands and a great bleeding lump on his forehead which he was trying to cover with his hat. There had been a cheap black bean rosary under him on the street which I had picked up and stuffed into his pocket as I pulled him to his feet, and he was clutching three crumpled dollar bills in one hand, and in the other, a bright yellow plastic bag obscenely stretched by what turned out to be a half gallon of cream sherry, miraculously unbroken (the reason he was out in the first place, or one reason, although there was no tell-tale smell of liquor on his breath).

I asked him where he lived, and reluctantly—"they mustn't know about this"—he admitted residence in a nursing home a few blocks away.

I volunteered to take him there by taxi but, no, he said, he would prefer to walk. He said he was missing his cane which he believed he had left in the liquor store off the corner where he had bought the sherry. He hadn't. The young man at the cash register said yes, he had been there not too long before but had left nothing behind. We looked along the counter and by the door. The young man gave me his card and asked with a distressed look in the old man's direction if there was anything else he could do? There obviously wasn't.

And so, the taxi once more refused, we tottered off down Third Avenue, Christ and me. It was Christ, of that I was convinced, heading for another liquor store where he had made his first visit and decided he could do better on the price. Indeed he had—saved twenty or twenty-five cents, he said bitterly.

We talked as we walked and I heard only some of his answers, spoken in a hesitant upstate murmur. He came from Cazenovia. He had a brother in Syracuse. He had been at the home for almost ten years. I revised my estimate of his age upward. What had he done before? He said something about the Christian brothers—whether he was one or simply lived with them, I couldn't make out. His mother had been 45 when he was born. He had had a sister who died of erysipelas. That was about it. He had a fit of trembling. Wanted to know how his forehead looked. Did it show? I tried to wipe the blood off but it kept coming. The angry knob was growing on his right temple. We pulled his hat still lower on his brow to cover it.

I offered a taxi again—a doctor—we could go to the hospital down the avenue. He refused with an emphasis reinforced by panic and stood straighter to demonstrate his recovery. We finally came to the liquor store he had visited earlier. I waited outside with the yellow plastic bag while he went in—he didn't want them to know that he had made his purchase elsewhere. No sign of the cane.

We went on another block or two, and avoiding the front entrance of the nursing home, rang the bell at the back door. Eventually someone came—an Irish attendant—not uniformed. He asked what had happened, where he'd been, not critical, but concerned. They had been worried. Francis—that was his name—asked to go to his room on thirteen and he wanted me to take him. No nonsense about the thirteenth floor being the fourteenth at this last stop before eternity. So I took him up to thirteen, past the expressions of tactful concern along the way, past the doors, open and shut, where other men and women, older and frailer, were waiting like Francis in a place that was quieter than a hospital, cleaner and brighter than an SRO hotel, for what came next.

He had a single room with bath, simple and comfortable, with a crucifix over the bed, holy pictures on the walls. He wanted to give me something for my trouble, groped in his pocket. I tried to tell him as gently as possible that it had been my pleasure, my opportunity to come to his assistance, that he had already given me much more than I deserved. But how do you tell Christ that he is Christ? You don't. You just consider the times you have been Christ yourself in the past and will be in the future, squeeze his shoulder in a gesture of reassurance and close the door gently behind you, leaving him sitting there on the edge of his bed still wearing his blood-stained hat.

PART III

Doctors and Doctoring

The Oath of Hippocrates

I swear by Apollo, the physician, and Asclepius and Health and All-Heal and all the gods and goddesses that, according to my ability and judgment, I will keep this oath and stipulation:

To reckon him who taught me this art equally dear to me as my parents, to share my substance with him and relieve his necessities if required; to regard his offspring as on the same footing with my own brothers, and to teach them this art if they should wish to learn it, without fee or stipulation, and that by precept, lecture and every other mode of instruction, I will impart a knowledge of the art to my own sons and to those of my teachers, and to disciples bound by a stipulation and oath, according to the law of medicine, but to none others.

I will follow that method of treatment which, according to my ability and judgment, I consider for the benefit of my patients, and abstain from whatever is deleterious and mischievous. I will give no deadly medicine to anyone if asked, nor suggest any such counsel; furthermore, I will not give to a woman an instrument to produce abortion.

With purity and with holiness I will pass my life and practice my art. I will not cut a person who is suffering from a stone, but will leave this to be done by practitioners of this work. Into whatever houses I enter I will go into them for the benefit of the sick and will abstain from every voluntary act of mischief and corruption; and further from the seduction of females or males, bond or free.

Whatever, in connection with my professional practice, or not in connection with it, I may see or hear in the lives of men which ought not to be spoken abroad I will not divulge, as reckoning that all such should be kept secret.

While I continue to keep this oath inviolate, may it be granted to me to enjoy life and the practice of the art, respected by all men at all times, but should I trespass and violate this oath, may the reverse be my lot.

On Death and Coding

RICHARD S. SANDOR, M.D.

I knew a sage once. He is thus far, the wisest man I've known. One night at dinner he asked me, "Do you read much?" "No," I confessed, "I used to, but now I read very little...I guess I don't believe I'm going to find what I'm looking for in books anymore." Tongue loosened by the fine Scotch he served, I went on, "Sometimes I'll even find myself having walked into a bookstore, but then almost immediately I begin to doubt that much will come of it, so I walk out without having looked at anything."

"I see," he said, "debilitating, that, giving up just as you've begun. You see, in truth, you really don't know why you are there. Perhaps there *is* a book you need to find or someone you're supposed to meet. Do you follow me?" And I nodded in agreement without being sure that I really did.

In time, I came to understand that he had diagnosed my condition as an early case of cynicism—the negative side of a new-found professionalism. It seems that in the process of mastering the enormous amount of material required to practice modern medicine, knowledge itself, once a haven from confusion, had become an instrument of bewilderment. I had taken an accidental overdose of information and had lost my appetite for the unknown.

The consequences of this knowledge-malaise became clear to me one day as I was sitting in the hospital cafeteria next to some interns on break from their duties in the Intensive Care Unit. In between bites of macaroni and cheese, they were talking about the tough day they were having. The more I tried to ignore their conversation, the more painfully aware of it I became. At the line, "And then this guy coded..." I was involuntarily launched out of my seat and across the room in horror.

I don't imagine there is a television viewer in America who doesn't know what the expression "Code Blue" means. Once upon a time, "Code Blue" was secret hospital language used to page a special team which would try to revive some unfortunate patient whose heart had stopped. Of course, now that everyone knows what it means, the phrase "Code Blue" has lost its power as a euphemism. But in their luncheon lament, those young doctors unwittingly revealed that what once hid the truth from the public, now concealed it from the professionals. Dying, once the central mystery of living, had become for them the trigger for a special job, a "Code Blue." Exactly what happens in the patient's experience at this moment isn't part of the phrase. *You* might be dying, but to us you are "coding," "have coded," or are "a code."

In all fairness, many grateful people have been revived from the brink of death by the "Code Blue" team—some of them have even been grateful to me. The problem is not that we have such powers but that we use them indiscriminately. Medical practice has become so complex that we've no choice but to reduce much of what we think or do to code, but then somewhere along the way we've forgotten what the code was invented for—why we practice medicine in the first place. One of the results is that, other than those who work in hospices, fewer and fewer of those who care for the ill know anything about death. We detect subtle disturbances of heart rhythm, manipulate faltering blood pressure to within a few millimeters of mercury, and regulate minute changes in blood chemistry, but what about the person who is dying?

My first encounter with death was different—perhaps just because I hadn't yet developed the professional armor that shields us from unanswered questions. I was taking part in a first-year medical school course called "The Doctor-Patient Relationship." A faction of our faculty, alarmed by the increasing disinterest among students in the *art* of medicine, put together a course in which we interviewed "real live" patients once a week. In the group sessions that followed these interviews, we shared our experiences while the faculty slipped in what they hoped would be antidotes to the deadening trends in medical education.

One Friday night, my assignment took me to the General Surgery floor of L.A. County Hospital to talk with an elderly man who'd been struck by a car. He was "under observation" (mine, as it turned out) with a preliminary diagnosis of pelvic fracture. Other, more urgent cases—mostly stab and gunshot wounds—were being whisked to and from the operating theater, hotly attended by the interns and residents. So my patient and I were pretty much left alone.

Mr. Francis wasn't having much pain—certainly not enough to require any "dope," he was quick to assure me. For a man of 64, he was in remarkably good shape. He explained that he owed his good health ("helt," he pronounced it) to the fact that he'd been a boxer in his youth and had maintained the habit of vigorous daily workouts. In addition, he'd eschewed the use of all drugs (prescribed and otherwise), didn't drink or smoke, ate gobs of lecithin studded with vitamin capsules ("You auta try some, Doc!"), and was careful about the types of ladies with whom he "...uh, well, ya know, go wit', Doc—hah!"

My "Doctor-Patient Relationship" interview couldn't have been easier or more pleasant. Mr. Francis regaled me with his stories of a life as foreign to me as the technological wizardry of County Hospital was to him. Several times he began a new tale with the line, "Now, let me tell you something, son..." I was entranced.

Suddenly in the midst of one of these stories, he paused, seemingly confused, and began to pick at the bed sheets—as though he couldn't get them quite right. Then, in a frightened voice, he said, "Hey, it's goin' dark in here—who's messin' wit' da lights?" As he started to try to climb over the bed-rails, I began to panic. What should I do? Stay at the bedside and keep him from falling out, or go for help? In the next moment he fell back into the bed unconscious and I ran to get the interns and residents. When we returned to the bedside, Mr. Francis was pale and still.

The gang of youthful saviors I'd summoned descended upon my friend with an almost voracious violence. And as they stabbed and pounded at Death, I backed away in guilty horror, because it was absolutely clear to me that the battle was already over. After twenty minutes of furious combat, they gave up, and my patient and I were once again alone. Amid the spattered blood, festooned by a tangle of tubes and wires, Mr. Francis looked for all the world like a great whale, harpooned and killed, ready for the flensing. I stood there, weeping in secret and thinking, "Where did he go?" One moment I'd been talking to a man—a lifetime of experience and memory, a way of talking and thinking and feeling, everything it takes to make a man—and then suddenly all that was gone. Where had it gone? I understood that the mangled carcass in the bed was just that, an empty container, but where were the contents?

Quietly, I removed all of the medical paraphernalia, arranged his body in the bed, closed his eyes, and propped his head up with a pillow so his jaw would not hang open. As I pulled a fresh sheet over him, his mouth moved and I jumped back in terror. Had they erred in pronouncing him dead? Quickly, I checked for a pulse, but there was none. Nor was there breath. I ran to tell an intern. With amused condescension he assured me that "reflex" movements like that could continue for as long as thirty minutes after death. So when do we die? I thought. Is awareness wrenched from its vessel in one piece or gradually? Did his consciousness remain in this realm until his body stopped moving? If so, Mr. Francis heard me say goodbye. For one thing was clear: life hadn't stopped, it had just gone somewhere else.

Like Mr. Francis, my father also died at the age of 64, but he never called me "son." I longed for him to. I wanted a wise and patient forester or fisherman for a father, and what I had instead was a brilliant and restless physician/investor who for years could reveal his pride in me only late at night and only to my mother (so she said).

Dad had a sign hung prominently in the living room: "If you're so smart, how come you ain't rich?" And as I look back, I realize I'd applied an alternate version of it to his life: "If you're so smart, how come you ain't happy?" But he was not at all malicious, only flawed, and he did his best. For a long time, I did not know how to love him. The passage of time and my own fatherhood softened the edges of our conflict, and we even learned to enjoy one another while collecting old and rare medical books.

One Saturday he called up wanting me to accompany him to a used book sale in a distant town (he didn't like going to such things alone), and in an uncharacteristic fit of selflessness, I decided not only to go with him, but also to give him my day. No matter what he told me to do, I would obey—a day of wholehearted service to my father.

Two minutes after we got on the freeway, he started. "Richard, get into the right lane." So I got over, simply, without argument inside or out. Several miles down the road he directed me to get off on what I believed to be the wrong exit, but I didn't argue with him. Twenty minutes later, we were lost. "Do you know how to get to this place?" he said. "Yes, I think so." "Well," (flustered arm waving) "go ahead— get us there." By the time we arrived, he was so shaken by my utter cooperation that he was almost out of instructions. But not quite. "Uh, well, why don't you go around that way, and I'll go this way. See what you find." I replied, "OK, Dad. Whatever you say."

Apparently, in addition to serving my father that day, I was meant to find a book. It turned out to be a first edition of Sir William Osler's *Principles and Practices of Medicine*. My father was ecstatic. As it was priced at 75 cents, we were getting the thing at a hundredth of its value. He was proud of me then, and it made me happy, but I also took my find as a sign from Above that my offering had been accept- ed. A little over a year later he died of leukemia.

I was with my father frequently towards the end. It was good to be able to care for him at last, but it was hard to watch his world shrink- ing. At first, he wanted to live to see his youngest child, my sister, graduate from college in June. Then he wanted to make it through the Christmas holidays. Then to Thanksgiving. The last time I was with him, he only wanted to get to the toilet and back under his own power.

There is a death in life the mystics speak of—the death of possessing in favor of being possessed. It's the lesson my wise friend was trying to convey to me at dinner that night. Twice, in attending dying men, what I believed I knew fell away. I saw that two worlds meet at death and that in dying we pass from one we know to another we don't. For Mr. Francis the journey was unexpected and abrupt. For my father it was inevitable and drawn out with pain.

It has been said that all medicines are poisons and that the difference between their power to heal or to destroy lies in dose. But what of the man who gives the medicine? Where is his measure?

Some Thoughts on Healing in Western Medicine

JOANNA M. WARD

Healing is not a word that is greatly used in Western medicine. We speak of wounds healing, or a healing touch, and we say that Time heals, but when it comes to our ordinary illnesses we often use the word "cure." In trying to assess the results of treatment we talk of the cure rate, of cancer for example, but more often we ask simply: "Are you better?" To get better—this already suggests that underneath we are not so sure of our state of health. Who, on being asked, "Are you well?" replies, "Yes, very well" with conviction? Children and the young, full of energy, will answer with a careless truth, but for most of us the conventional reply: "Very well, thank you" is accompanied by doubt. We may know which part of us is ailing—that it is our joints which ache, or that we are too fat—but in addition, there is some sense of lack. How we really are is not always clear, and perhaps it is significant that the word healing—"to make whole"—is now more often reserved for spiritual or alternative methods of medicine, with an unconscious admission of this lack in our orthodox Western medicine.

Healing is primarily a natural function of living tissues, and the human body is very well adapted to heal itself. It contains intricate mechanisms to maintain metabolic balance and to regulate the internal temperature of the body or the purity of the blood and hormone levels against all the natural forces both inside and outside the body which tend to destabilize. We shiver when we are cold, we sweat when we are hot, we become thirsty in dry conditions. The body can also fight infections, often very successfully, and it fights cancer, although less successfully. Above all it heals wounds. The whole of modern surgery is dependent upon this healing power. With whatever skill diseased or damaged tissue is removed, replaced, and stitched up, healing finally depends entirely upon this innate capacity of tissues to regenerate and knit together, to remake the whole. This *vis mediatrix naturae* spoken of by the Greeks is a truly great power.

As a dermatologist, I freeze a wart on a patient's thumb with liquid nitrogen. I carefully explain that the condition is fundamentally self-healing, and that, providing it has already been there for some time, my treatment is likely to cure. I know in fact that only eight out of ten of these cases will be healed and that the process is a mixture of physical destruction, the power of my suggestion, and the natural tendency of the body to overcome the wart virus. I do not know which two out of the ten cases will relapse or fail to heal.

A good deal of the work of medical doctors proceeds in this way. In dermatology there are myriads of small problems, perhaps because the skin is so visible. People come with blemishes, minor infections, transient rashes, small skin cancers, or "something not right" with the hair or nails. The free health service in England has encouraged people to take these problems to their doctor, and so similar situations occur in every specialty. Much or our time in Western medicine is spent in dealing with such matters quite satisfactorily.

In the Orient, this treatment of symptoms is considered a very low form of medicine, but perhaps it corresponds to the way we live. We have to accept that our Western civilization with all its artificiality, complexity, and stress contributes to the superficiality of our medical practices. There is not enough time, with so many patients to see, to take in the person who comes with the wart—perhaps it is not necessary. We live on the outside, superficially, always in a hurry, with no patience, and lacking the stoicism of past ages. It is different in the Third World where, although the lack of modern medicine is felt keenly, the older methods of the medicine man still have their place and there is a greater acceptance of suffering.

The real challenge which doctors must face are the chronic problems, many of which tend to beset us as we get older. They often represent a failure in the functioning of different organs: rise in blood pressure, chronic stomach ulcers, arthritis, deafness, over-stretched lungs, diabetes, strokes, Parkinson's disease. Other problems, such as asthma and eczema, appear early in life. Some of these conditions run in families, such as a tendency to high blood pressure, eczema, and psoriasis, and some are frankly degenerative. But it seems likely that they represent some state of imbalance in the body as a whole which results finally in breakdown at a site which may be predetermined by heredity. There are many internal and external factors which may take part in this breakdown: questions of diet, drink, the pace of modern life, and what we call "stress." The way in which I take the difficulties of my life may be quite different from the way another faces the same problems. Our lives need to be seen as a whole, including job, family, and perhaps even fate.

The fact is that we do know an enormous amount about these diseases in Western medicine, and perhaps this tends to obscure our fundamental ignorance. It is difficult for the layman to appreciate the extent and detail of modern medical research and how much *is* known. With the use of increasingly complex techniques we know a great deal. We have worked out the intricate mechanisms of the changes occurring in diseases, and volumes upon volumes of research pour out.

But very often we know *how* and not *why* these changes occur. It is as if we were examining in minute detail the leaves of a great tree without the perception that they are part of a whole and are attached to twigs and to branches and thence unified in one trunk. The roots of disease remain unknown. We do not know why our patients become ill now, at a particular moment in their life. We do not know, for example, why any one patient gets Parkinson's disease, although we know with great exactitude the degenerative changes which cause it. We may know the mechanics of the symptoms, but in many skin diseases we do not even know that. Why do the different rashes appear in such constant and bizarre patterns, only affecting knees and elbows, for example, so that the diagnosis is as instantly recognizable to a dermatologist as are plants to a botanist?

This is not to say that we cannot ameliorate and even treat many of these diseases. We have developed an amazing battery of weapons to attack the causes of disease according to our knowledge. Some are very effective, as in the replacement of thyroid hormones in patients who have become deficient in it, or the use of insulin to treat diabetes. Vast numbers of drugs are used to regulate wrong functioning of the heart, lungs, and bowels, with varying success, partly because of unwanted side-effects and partly because we are treating the symptoms rather than the underlying causes. Our medicine was transformed with the introduction of penicillin and later other antibiotics to attack infections, many of which were previously life threatening, such as those of infancy and old age and the very dangerous ones associated with childbirth. The drugs have many side-effects when used long-term. And now, for cancer and many other major disorders, immunosuppressive drugs are found to be very effective, but, by definition, they depress the body's own fighting or immune system. Nevertheless, Western medicine can save the life of a child with leukemia by using these drugs, and it is doubtful whether any Oriental treatment can do this.

It is difficult to keep a sense of perspective between the triumphs of Western medicine and its failings. No one who has experienced the marvels of modern surgery—the painless hip after years of pain, or the fresh life after surgery for angina—can doubt the capabilities of such science. But there remain a great number of people with chronic ailments for which we have no cure. We can offer some symptomatic relief and we can try to give support in the situation as a whole, but fundamentally we are unable to alter the course of the disease.

There are also other dimensions involved in this question of healing and one of these is the human transaction. What does the doctor represent? Gone are the days when the doctor was a distinguished visitor, a highly respected member of the community. Gone also, more or less, are the days of the big chief with the correspondingly big ego.

Recently, fresh value has been given to the doctor/patient relationship, and in some ways things have improved, especially in the field of family medicine. In hospitals, despite much effort and increasing modernity, there is often less sense of service. In the past, and still in a few centers, everyone who worked in a hospital took pride in it and there was respect for the sick. As a patient, one knows how important every transaction is in this vulnerable situation, whether it be with porter, radiologist, nurse, or doctor. The heart has its needs and the psyche can heal. We all know there are good doctors, doctors with wisdom, who do indeed help us to bear our situation, and that there are also those who are less good. Some with highly trained intellects or perhaps great surgical skill are lacking in feeling. Similarly, patients vary from the remarkably courageous, who will do everything in their power to help their own healing, to the frankly neurotic.

Personally I am reluctant to think of myself as a healer, due to a sense of inadequacy and an awareness of the mechanicity and coarseness of the relationship with my patients, which is pierced by moments of warmth and sympathy. These facts cannot be denied. At best I try to bring my intuitive/instinctive perception, borne of long experience, to this particular patient, and to include in this consideration not only the apparent diagnosis but to some extent the very nature of this person and his or her life, and then to bring the best treatment, again learned through long experience, that my training in orthodox medicine suggests. One prays above all for an open heart through which something may pass which can truly help the situation—a sense of care and of understanding. For real healing, I am convinced, requires a higher understanding and a higher power. It becomes plain that standing on the flat earth surrounded by our data we are limited in our vision. It could only be by a true growth in stature that we would see and understand further.

One of the characteristics of Western medicine is the importance we put upon accurate diagnosis as a prelude to treatment. We believe we cannot treat without this "naming," and in truth it is obvious that if I have no idea what is the matter I cannot treat a patient. But, it encourages a tendency to trust too much this fact of labelling, and we lose sight of the patient as a whole. In fact the process may stop at the labelling. We say: "You have bronchitis" and everyone is satisfied. We are trained to take a detailed story from every patient which will include his present and past illnesses and details of family and social problems. We are also trained to examine the whole body thoroughly. Yet at the level at which we practice, this information does not add up to a whole.

It is very salutary to attend a homeopath and find that he arrives at his diagnosis, and therefore treatment, by an entirely different set of questions, as though he were examining a different segment of the whole, and in consequence he can help certain things that we cannot help. But an entire world of interventional medicine exists, including life-saving surgical procedures, which pass the homeopath by and which he sometimes seems to ignore in his overview of the situation. It is perhaps part of the same weakness that affects us all, a weakness in our capacity to see things on a bigger scale, and in our smallness we deny the place of other traditions.

Visiting a Chinese doctor for treatment with herbs and acupuncture is yet another experience. Again the questions are different, but more remarkable is the diagnosis of disease by looking at the tongue and taking the pulse. It is very humbling for us to learn that there are four or five different types of pulse and to realize the fineness of diagnosis accessible to this tradition which goes back 3000 years, so much further than ours. Chinese medicine detects abnormalities in the flow of the vital life force, then attempts to restore the balance through acupuncture, the use of which has always been closely related to spiritual powers, relating to a vision of the human being as the container not only of organs, but also of finer energies. Western medicine is astonishingly arrogant in its dismissal of these age-old traditions. Although there is an increasing interest in these methods of healing among family doctors, they are still rejected outright by most hospital practitioners in the United Kingdom—perhaps because they are felt to challenge the whole scientific basis upon which our medicine stands, and because they deal with things which cannot be measured by our methods. Even where evidence for the success of acupuncture and Chinese herbs is irrefutable, we make great efforts to prove that they must work by some other mechanisms more acceptable to us, and that the herbs must contain some "wonder drug" previously unknown to us. From an early point in our training, strong conditioning to believe only what we see and can measure physically prevents us from trusting our other perceptions. Science does indeed blind us.

On the other hand, the almost total rejection of modern medicine by many exponents of so-called complementary medicine is equally blinkered. Many of these therapies are plainly peripheral to the central understanding of Oriental medicine, and although they may be part of the great tree which remains hidden from us all, blind faith and lack of discrimination do not help understanding.

There is another great area of divergence, that between psychology and general medicine. The psyche has long been respectable in America and only more recently so in England—in my early days as a doctor I remember being told by a well-known dermatologist that "the psyche was all bunk." There is still a certain division between the general physician and the psychiatrist: their worlds tend to be mysterious to each other. Yet in everyday life few of us would deny how much we have been influenced by our upbringing, and that we love, hate, and feel jealousy and joy—all experiences inconveniently immeasurable.

These dimensions seem to remain hidden and can be ignored just as we ignore the fact that many of us believe in the possibility of religious experience. Religious experience, in different forms, has pervaded human history since its origins. How fine would be the scales that could measure the emotions, let alone the love of God! Maybe real healing belongs to just such an order of experience.

In the end, are there not levels of healing, levels of the body and of the psyche of which we have spoken, and beyond? Is there not a healing force from on high which may visit us if we are prepared? Though they are rarely found, there are men and women of true stature and training who can mediate such forces. They are spoken of in all traditions—and the result will be what it will be.

Word-Salad

MILTON H. ERICKSON

In dealing with any type of patient clinically, there is a most important consideration which should be kept constantly in mind. This is that the patient's needs as a human personality should be an ever-present question for the therapist to insure recognition at each manifestation. Merely to make a correct diagnosis of the illness and to know the correct method of treatment is not enough. Fully as important is that the patient be receptive of the therapy and cooperative in regard to it. Without the patient's full cooperativeness, therapeutic results are delayed, distorted, limited, or even prevented. Too often the therapist regards the patient as necessarily logical, understanding, in full possession of his faculties, in brief, a reasonable and informed human being. Yet it is a matter of common knowledge often overlooked, disregarded or rejected that a patient can be silly, forgetful, absurd, unreasonable, illogical, incapable of acting with common sense, and very often governed and directed in his behavior by emotions and unknown, unrecognizable, and perhaps undiscoverable unconscious needs and forces which are far from reasonable, logical, or sensible. Too often it is not the strengths of the person that are vital in the therapeutic situation. Rather, the dominant forces that control the entire situation may derive from weaknesses, illogical behavior,

118

unreasonableness, and obviously false and misleading attitudes of various sorts.

The therapist wishing to help his patient should never scorn, condemn nor reject any part of a patient's conduct simply because it is obstructive, unreasonable or even irrational. Sometimes, in fact, many more times than is realized, therapy can be firmly established on a sound basis only by the utilization of silly, absurd, irrational, and contradictory manifestations. One's professional dignity is not involved but one's professional competence is. To illustrate from clinical experience, I will cite a case history.

George had been a patient in a mental hospital for five years. His identity had never been established. He was simply a stranger around the age of twenty-five who had been picked up by the police for irrational behavior and committed to the state mental hospital. During those five years he had said, "My name is George," "Good morning," and "Good night," but these were his only rational utterances. He uttered otherwise a continuous word-salad completely meaningless as far as could be determined. It was made up of sounds, syllables, words, and incomplete phrases. For the first three years he sat on a bench at the front door of the ward and eagerly leaped up and poured forth his word-salad most urgently to everyone who entered the ward. Otherwise, he merely sat quietly mumbling his word-salad to himself. Innumerable efforts had been made by psychiatrists, psychologists, nurses, social service workers, other personnel and even fellow patients to secure intelligible remarks from him, all in vain. George talked only one way, the word-salad way. After approximately three years he continued to greet persons who entered the ward with an outburst of meaningless words, but in between times he sat silently on the bench, appearing mildly depressed but somewhat angrily uttering a few minutes of word-salad when approached and questioned.

The author joined the hospital staff in the sixth year of George's stay. The available information about his ward behavior was secured. It was learned also that patients or ward personnel could sit on the bench beside him without eliciting his word-salad so long as they did not speak to him. With this total of information a therapeutic plan was devised. A secretary recorded in shorthand the word-salads with which he so urgently greeted those who entered the ward. These transcribed recordings were studied but no meaning could be discovered. These word-salads were carefully paraphrased, using words that were least likely to be found in George's productions and an extensive study was made of these until the author could improvise a word-salad similar in pattern to George's, but utilizing a different vocabulary.

Then all entrances to the ward were made through a side door some distance down the corridor from George. The author then began the practice of sitting silently on the bench beside George daily for increasing lengths of time until the span of an hour was reached. Then, at the next sitting, the author, addressing the empty air, identified himself verbally. George made no response.

The next day the identification was addressed directly to George. He spat out an angry stretch of word-salad to which the author replied, in tones of courtesy and responsiveness, with an equal amount of his own carefully contrived word-salad. George appeared puzzled and, when the author finished, George uttered another contribution with an inquiring intonation. As if replying the author verbalized still further word-salad.

After a half dozen interchanges, George lapsed into silence and the author promptly went about other matters.

The next morning appropriate greetings were exchanged, employing proper names by both. Then George launched into a long word-salad speech to which the author courteously replied in kind. There followed then brief interchanges of long and short utterances of word-salad until George fell silent and the author went to other duties.

This continued for some time. Then George, after returning the morning greeting, made meaningless utterances without pause for four hours. It taxed the author greatly to miss lunch and make a full reply in kind. George listened attentively and made a two-hour reply to which a weary two-hour response was made. (George was noted to watch the clock throughout the day.)

The next morning George returned the usual greeting properly but added about two sentences of nonsense to which the author replied with a similar length of nonsense. George replied, "Talk sense, Doctor." "Certainly, I'll be glad to. What is your last name?"

"O'Donovan and it's about time somebody who knows how to talk asked. Over five years in this lousy joint"...(to which was added a sentence or two of word-salad). The author replied, "I'm glad to get your name, George. Five years is too long a time"...(and about two sentences of word-salad were added).

The rest of the account is as might be expected. A complete history sprinkled with bits of word-salad was obtained by inquiries judiciously salted with word-salad. His clinical course, never completely free of word-salad which was eventually reduced to occasional unintelligible mumbles, was excellent. Within a year he had left the hospital, was gainfully employed, and at increasingly longer intervals returned to the hospital to report his continued and improving adjustment. Nevertheless, he invariably initiated his report or terminated it with a bit of word-salad, always expecting the same from the author. Yet he could, as he frequently did on these visits, comment wryly, "Nothing like a little nonsense in life, is there, Doctor?" to which he obviously expected and received a sensible expression of agreement to which was added a brief utterance of nonsense. After he had been out of the hospital continuously for three years of fully satisfactory adjustment, contact was lost with him except for a cheerful postcard from another city. This bore a brief but satisfactory summary of his adjustments in a distant city. It was signed properly but following his name was a jumble of syllables. There was no return address. He was ending the relationship on his terms of adequate understanding.

The above case represents a rather extreme example of meeting a patient at the level of his decidedly serious problem. The author was at first rather censoriously criticized by others but when it became apparent that inexplicable imperative needs of the patient were being met, there was no further adverse comment.

Including Even Our Mad Parts

Ann Belford Ulanov

Our task, individually and socially, is to make space for all the gaps in our being, and thus to include even the mad parts. We must face how hard we make it in our society for our mad parts to speak and to be. Either individuals are drugged in mental hospitals, going without speaking for weeks, or by an act of a legislature are dumped back onto city streets, unhoused and unheard, despite their yelling out at us at street corners. Madness, like health, is a way of living in both inner and outer worlds. If we do not make space for it, it will translate itself into homicide, suicide, every physical symptom, all the terrors, like the amassing of pressures around the heart, or the amassing of weapons in countries. It will reduce itself like the translation of complexities into oversimplified ultimatums of the "all or nothing" variety—diet plans, unbreakable prayer schedules, the dictated conditions that must precede people sitting down at peace tables.

It is this self, concrete, mad and sane, this sense of I-ness, that touches God and that God touches.

What is this touching like? It is pain and it is joy.

We not only may seek, we are forced to seek that concrete sense of I-ness in touch with the transcendent through the compulsion of illness, obsessive fantasy, entrapping depression, or disintegrating anxiety. We can be brought to a sense of I-ness through health or madness, but not through that conformity where we forsake our vocation or turn away from the summons to be in the concrete place before us with its concrete tasks. The parts of ourselves and of our world press to be gathered in, to be made into self and world. To refuse that gathering and the tasks it imposes is to turn from the will of God that wants to be realized right here in the doubt and insecurity of our concrete self and concrete world. We are called to accept without reservations the particular concrete situation in which we find ourselves, to consent to make order in the chaos into which we are born. That is our cross and we must carry it.

To try to gather all these parts means pain, because some of the parts are missing, some even lost, a few banished. To set out to collect them means looking for the thing in ourselves we despised or feared, the thing in the world we avoided. It feels like opening a door to a horde of barbarians, to the beast in the garden, to all the crude, unthinking, impulsive needs, dreads, and hurts hiding in the unconscious. That is painful. Even more painful is what follows, because when unconscious contents become conscious, they transform themselves into concrete tasks and obligations. Here is an example.

A man dreamt that he was present at the crucifixion of Jesus: "I could not see but I could hear. And I heard Jesus yelling out and cursing in his agony of suffering. I was afraid. I thought, they never tell you this part. I felt I was admitted to an awesome secret." For the dreamer, the Christ figure was doing what the dreamer needed to do and was avoiding—to register consciously his pain, the yelling and cursing pain itself, and with it the outrage that such a pain could exist. This was the missing part for the dreamer. This was the pain he was avoiding. For he was undergoing the death and rebirth of his whole religious orientation. But he wanted to duck the suffering, to repress it, which only paralyzed his actions. He rationalized his experience as not important, because he was there to serve others, which paralyzed his emotions and foisted his unconscious pain onto others around him, far from serving them. His task was to take up his missing part and feel it, to submit to his own pain.

This task confronts all of us, to deal with what touches us and not avoid it, to collect our missing parts, the neglected and overlooked and banished parts of our inner and outer populations. We are never touched in the abstract, only in the flesh. The marks of our own frown lines, our overweight, our sleepless nights, our neighborhood crime, our neglected land or polluted air reveal this truth. God waits in those parts, waits for us to visit the part left in the prison of repression, waits for us to offer some life-giving water to outcast sexual parts, to give food to starving parts. All these bits must be gathered in and nourished. As Lady Julian of Norwich puts it, all must be knit in, must be one with God.

So the first avenue of pain leads to our opening up to our outcast parts, to our learning to make room for the mad bits, the gaps, like the dreamer with the beast, needing to find room for its prowling savagery.

A second avenue of pain opens from the first, from our weakened defenses. When we try to collect all the parts of ourselves and our world into consciousness, we can no longer so easily protect ourselves through denial of the suffering around us and within us. We can no longer succeed in blocking out what is there. We cannot split away from it. We cannot disown what is painful as if it did not touch us. Now we are touched. We can see what others go through. The hungry child of another continent bears our own child's face. We can no longer just blame our neighbor for everything, saying, in effect, the beast is yours, not mine. The stone we cast hits us as well. We see how we are all touched by evil and how we must struggle to help one another. Our old opaqueness to suffering is diluted to a palpable transparency and our pain increases.

How odd and how paradoxical! Our work, in order to receive all parts of our psyche without segregating any, both liberates and unifies us. It makes us stronger, yet also delivers us into pain. For now we feel more immediately what we go through, and what other people endure, all of which opens us to more pain, and to more grace, as we disidentify from any and all of the parts. Being open now to the whole, to including all the parts, detaches us from the false security of identifying with any one of the parts as if it were the whole truth.

Healer Within

Norman Cousins

What can we learn from patients who have recovered from supposedly irreversible illnesses, including malignancies, cardiac infirmities,
and diseases of the joints and muscles? Is there anything in these
recoveries that might be useful to others similarly afflicted?

For the past ten years, I've had the opportunity to meet with a significant number of such patients. In talking with them, I was reminded that Hippocrates viewed the treatment of disease as a dual process.
One part was represented by systematic medicine; the other part was
the full activation of the patient's own healing system. In the centuries since the great physician taught his students under the
sycamore tree on the Greek island of Kos, there has been a shift away
from the concept of the patient as the center of the healing process.
The physician has come increasingly to the fore as the dominant
force.

The patients I studied, however, were not content to be passive
participants in their own illnesses. Most of them were told, when the
diagnosis of illness was made, that the chances for recovery were slim.
Unfortunately, a significant number of these patients experienced a
severe downturn following the diagnosis. Some of them suffered from
panic and depression, not uncommon reactions to serious disease.

Many cancer patients, for instance, report difficulty sleeping—a difficulty that stems as much from their fear as from their pain.

Similarly, some heart attack patients never reach the hospital alive, not just because of the condition itself, but because panic may cause further constriction of the blood vessels, imposing an intolerable additional burden. Brain research is now turning up evidence that attitudes of defeat or panic not only constrict the blood vessels, but create emotional stresses that have a debilitating effect on the endocrine and immune systems. Conversely, attitudes of confidence and determination activate benevolent and therapeutic secretions in the brain.

One patient I worked with briefly, whom I'll call Sheila, provided a dramatic example of the importance of the mind in the recovery process. When I first met her, she was a thirty-four-year-old woman facing a mastectomy for life-threatening breast cancer. She was reluctant to have the operation, feeling that male doctors are too casual in suggesting that women have their breasts removed. Based on what I knew of her case, I urged her to have the surgery, and spoke to her about the importance of having high expectations going into the operating room—of seeing the surgery as a chance to free her body from an offender, rather than the beginning of a downward spiral toward death. We talked for a while about the studies that have given a scientific basis to the anecdotal stories of the mind's power in fighting illness, and she thanked me and left.

She decided to go ahead with the surgery, but a week or so later her physician called me to say the operation had been canceled. The tumor, which the doctor had described to me earlier as "a hand grenade," had disappeared entirely. Sheila was taking no medication at the time; the only explanation is that her own cancer-fighting capability had risen to the occasion, with the full array of immune cells that produce the body's own chemotherapy and infuse it into the cancer cells.

While not every story is as remarkable as Sheila's, most of the patients I studied made a conscious decision, when their spiraling panic and illness reached a point of desperation, to reject all notions of inevitability. They became determined not to rely exclusively on treatment provided by others, but to take an active part in the quest for recovery. They accepted the physician's diagnosis and the unfavorable odds that came along with it, but refused to be deterred by the accompanying prediction of doom

All of them were, in their own way, living out an ancient idea that is coming back into favor through current medical research—the idea that the healing system is connected to a belief system, that attitudes play a vital part in the recovery process. The medical community has acknowledged the human brain's ability to exercise a measure of control over the autonomic nervous system, and as a result is paying renewed attention to the patient's role in overcoming disease and maintaining good health.

Clearly, in our modern age, treatment for any disease requires the best that medical science has to offer; all the emotional determination in the world usually falls short without prompt and consistent medical intervention. But just as clearly, treating physical illness without paying corresponding attention to emotional needs can have only a partial effect.

More than 2,000 years after the death of Hippocrates, we are coming back to the original Hippocratic ideal of the patient not as a passive vessel into which the physician pours therapeutic skills and medicaments, but as a sovereign human being capable of generating powerful responses to disease. These powerful responses won't reverse every incidence of disease or illness; otherwise, we would live forever. But by beginning to recognize these powers, we are enhancing vital elements of the recovery process.

Spiritus Contra Spiritum

THE BILL WILSON / CARL JUNG LETTERS

January 23, 1961

My dear Dr. Jung:

This letter of great appreciation has been very long overdue.

May I first introduce myself as Bill Wilson, a co-founder of the Society of Alcoholics Anonymous. Though you have surely heard of us, I doubt if you are aware that a certain conversation you once had with one of your patients, a Mr. Roland H., back in the early 1930's, did play a critical role in the founding of our Fellowship.

Though Roland H. has long since passed away, the recollection of his remarkable experience while under treatment by you has definitely become part of AA history. Our remembrance of Roland H.'s statements about his experience with you is as follows:

Having exhausted other means of recovery from his alcoholism, it was about 1931 that he became your patient. I believe he remained under your care for perhaps a year. His admiration for you was boundless, and he left you with a feeling of much confidence. To his great consternation, he soon relapsed into intoxication. Certain that you were his "court of last resort," he again returned to your care. Then followed the conversation between you that was to become the first link in the chain of events that led to the founding of Alcoholics Anonymous.

My recollection of his account of that conversation is this: First of all, you frankly told him of his hopelessness, so far as any further medical or psychiatric treatment might be concerned. This candid and humble statement of yours was beyond doubt the first foundation stone upon which our Society has since been built.

Coming from you, one he so trusted and admired, the impact upon him was immense.

When he then asked you if there was any other hope, you told him that there might be, provided he could become the subject of a spiritual or religious experience—in short, a genuine conversion. You pointed out how such an experience, if brought about, might remotivate him when nothing else could. But you did caution, though, that while such experiences had sometimes brought recovery to alcoholics, they were, nevertheless, comparatively rare. You recommended that he place himself in a religious atmosphere and hope for the best. This I believe was the substance of your advice.

Shortly thereafter, Mr. H. joined the Oxford Group, an evangelical movement that was then at the height of its success in Europe, and one with which you are doubtless familiar. You will remember their large emphasis upon the principles of self-survey, confession, restitution, and the giving of oneself in service to others. They strongly stressed meditation and prayer. In these surroundings, Roland H. did find a conversion experience that released him for the time being from his compulsion to drink.

Returning to New York, he became very active with the "O.G." here, then led by an Episcopal clergyman, Dr. Samuel Shoemaker. Dr. Shoemaker had been one of the founders of that movement, and his was a powerful personality that carried immense sincerity and conviction.

At this time (1932–1934), the Oxford Group had already sobered a number of alcoholics, and Roland, feeling that he could especially identify with these sufferers, addressed himself to the help of still others. One of these chanced to be an old schoolmate of mine, named Edwin T. ["Ebby"]. He had been threatened with commitment to an institution, but Mr. H. and another ex–alcoholic "O.G." member procured his parole, and helped to bring about his sobriety.

Meanwhile, I had run the course of alcoholism and was threatened with commitment myself. Fortunately, I had fallen under the care of a physician—a Dr. William D. Silkworth—who was wonderfully capable of understanding alcoholics. But just as you had given up on Roland, so had he given me up. It was his theory that alcoholism had two components—an obsession that compelled the sufferer to drink against his will and interest, and some sort of metabolism difficulty which he then called an allergy. The alcoholic's compulsion guaranteed that the alcoholic's drinking would go on, and the allergy made sure that the sufferer would finally deteriorate, go insane, or die. Though I had been one of the few he had thought it possible to help, he was finally obliged to tell me of my hopelessness; I, too, would have to be locked up. To me, this was a shattering blow. Just as Roland had been made ready for his conversion experience by you, so had my wonderful friend Dr. Silkworth prepared me.

Hearing of my plight, my friend Edwin T. came to see me at my home, where I was drinking. By then, it was November 1934. I had long marked my friend Edwin for a hopeless case. Yet here he was in a very evident state of "release," which could by no means be accounted for by his mere association for a short time with Oxford Group. Yet this obvious state of release, as distinguished from the usual depression, was tremendously convincing. Because he was a kindred sufferer, he could unquestionably communicate with me at great depth. I knew at once I must find an experience like his, or die.

Again I returned to Dr. Silkworth's care, where I could be once more sobered and so gain a clearer view of my friend's experience of release, and of Roland H.'s approach to him.

Clear once more of alcohol, I found myself terribly depressed. This seemed to be caused by my inability to gain the slightest faith. Edwin T. again visited me and repeated the simple Oxford Group formulas. Soon after he left me, I became even more depressed. In utter despair, I cried out, "If there be a God, will He show Himself." There immediately came to me an illumination of enormous impact and dimension, something which I have since tried to describe in the book *Alcoholics Anonymous* and also in *AA Comes of Age*, basic texts which I am sending to you.

My release from the alcohol obsession was immediate. At once, I knew I was a free man.

Shortly following my experience, my friend Edwin came to the hospital, bringing me a copy of William James's *Varieties of Religious Experience*. This book gave me the realization that most conversion experiences, whatever their variety, do have a common denominator of ego collapse at depth. The individual faces an impossible dilemma. In my case, the dilemma had been created by my compulsive drinking, and the deep feeling of hopelessness had been vastly deepened still more by my alcoholic friend when he acquainted me with your verdict of hopelessness respecting Roland H.

In the wake of my spiritual experience, there came a vision of a society of alcoholics, each identifying with and transmitting his experience to the next—chain-style. If each sufferer were to carry the news of the scientific hopelessness of alcoholism to each new prospect, he might be able to lay every newcomer wide open to a transforming spiritual experience. This concept proved to be the foundation of such success as Alcoholics Anonymous has since achieved. This has made conversion experiences—nearly every variety reported by James—available on almost a wholesale basis. Our sustained recoveries over the last quarter-century number about 300,000. In America and through the world, there are today 8,000 AA groups.*

So to you, to Dr. Shoemaker of the Oxford Group, to William James, and to my own physician, Dr. Silkworth, we of AA owe this tremendous benefaction. As you will now clearly see, this astonishing chain of events actually started long ago in your consulting room, and it was directly founded upon your own humility and deep perception.

Very many thoughtful AAs are students of your writings. Because of your conviction that man is something more than intellect, emotion, and two dollars' worth of chemicals, you have especially endeared yourself to us....

Please be certain that your place in the affection, and in the history, of our Fellowship is like no other.

Gratefully yours,
William G. Wilson

Editor's note: As of 1993, worldwide membership was estimated to be 2,048,955; number of groups, over 89,215.

January 30, 1961

Dear Mr. Wilson:

Your letter has been very welcome indeed.

I had no news from Roland H. any more and often wondered what has been his fate. Our conversation which he has adequately reported to you had an aspect of which he did not know. The reason that I could not tell him everything was that those days I had to be exceedingly careful of what I said. I had found out that I was misunderstood in every possible way. Thus I was very careful when I talked to Roland H. But what I really thought about was the result of many experiences with men of his kind.

His craving for alcohol was the equivalent, on a low level, of the spiritual thirst of our being for wholeness; expressed in medieval language: the union with God.

How could one formulate such an insight in a language that is not misunderstood in our days?

The only right and legitimate way to such an experience is that it happens to you in reality, and it can only happen to you when you walk on a path which leads you to higher understanding. You might be led to that goal by an act of grace or through a personal and honest contact with friends, or through a higher education of the mind beyond the confines of mere rationalism. I see from your letter that Roland H. has chosen the second way, which was, under the circumstances, obviously the best one.

I am strongly convinced that the evil principle prevailing in this world leads the unrecognized spiritual need into perdition if it is not counteracted either by real religious insight or by the protective wall of human community. An ordinary man, not protected by an action from above and isolated in society, cannot resist the power of evil, which is called very aptly the Devil. But the use of such words arouses so many mistakes that one can only keep aloof from them as much as possible.

These are the reasons why I could not give a full and sufficient explanation to Roland H., but I am risking it with you because I conclude from your very decent and honest letter that you have acquired a point of view above the misleading platitudes one usually hears about alcoholism.

You see, "alcohol" in Latin is *spiritus*, and we use the same word for the highest religious experience as well as for the most depraving poison. The helpful formula therefore is: *spiritus contra spiritum.* Thanking you again for your kind letter,

I remain
yours sincerely
C.G. Jung

PART IV

Medicine
East and West

A Meeting of Traditional Tibetan and Western Medicine

A Conversation Between Keith Cohn and Lobsang Rapgay

KEITH COHN: When I was growing up, the most extraordinary things we heard of were in the scientific field—the discovery of penicillin, polio eradication, x-ray. And yet, as wondrous as such discoveries were, they were something a young person could aspire to understand. Everything could eventually be known, even mastered—the mystery and magic had been taken from our world. I mention "magic" here because I think "healing" involves a touch of magic—the inexplicable and wonderful. So we start with a confusing situation: on one hand science was intrinsically fascinating to the young, curious mind, and yet scientific questions were "known" to be solvable. We were living in the Age of Reason, and that meant we were to take command of nature, and of nature's diseases. The miraculous had been brought down to the level required to fix any problem. This is probably a typical background of most Western doctors. How does this compare with your own experiences; what was the relationship in your life between the "extraordinary" and the explosion of modern technology and information?

LOBSANG RAPGAY: The Tibetans have always maintained a very open attitude toward different points of view and incorporated ideas from many different cultures and times. I grew up with the magic of the ancient Bon people, the spirits, demons, and deities from the Buddhist teachings. And Tibetan medicine came from the far reaches of India, China, Persia, and Greece. So you see in Tibetan Buddhist thought and in the origin of Tibetan medicine there has always been an interplay between the mysterious and the concrete. The Buddhist world neither negates nor agrees with the Western world view: you have the middle path, where you learn Western thought at one level, and at another, internal, level you feel that here are many areas which cannot be understood or explained purely from a sensory, perceptive level.

KC: Yes, whereas our picture of how the world is put together rests on the most up-to-date scientific facts—these have always been "dependable" and "real" for us. You know, for years I hardly wondered about the foundations of modern biomedicine—how was it that, millions of years before, life simply bubbled up out of a melange of lifeless molecules and chemicals—entirely accidentally, and without any meaningful rhyme or reason? And once set into motion, living beings seem to churn along according to fairly predictable, physical laws and processes—just as any other gadget? Without knowing it, we had deified our scientific discoveries—submitted to their "reign of quantity." If we need to know anything more about the objective world out there, we simply run a series of measurements and analyses.

LR: Whereas the basic Buddhist viewpoint holds that external reality is closely intertwined with our perception of it. Buddhism would say that though an actual, external world does exist, what we know of its existence remains closely interrelated with out perception of it. In Tibetan thought (and medicine) you see an interplay between the two—the external world is inseparable from the mind.

KC: And then we turn to Western medicine, where illness, by and large, is considered a chance circumstance—someone just happens to inherit a disease, become exposed to a virus, develop a malignancy.

As doctors, we become so absorbed in getting rid of a disease, we seldom stop and ask what it is telling us—what we know of its source or meaning. Rather than thinking of an illness as just an unfortunate happening, would it not be more accurate to consider it an expression of what our life has brought us to—how cut off we are from the deeper sources of our being? Just as global warming speaks to the desecration of our environment, does not an illness signal our failure to attend our own natural forces and energies? This idea becomes a delicate one, because we don't want to cast blame or feed the useless guilt so often accompanying an illness. And we both know many disorders appear haphazardly, without a definable cause....

LR: ...outside the purview of personal involvement, accidentally or synchronistically—from phenomena or forces much greater and universal than any of our small lives.

KC: Yes, we agree, but excluding that for a moment, I am asking whether human illness arises—as we believe in the modern era—from some singular cause or faulty part, such as a broken bone or cholesterol, or whether our maladies don't oftentimes reflect who and what we are? From this perspective we see that a real physician would have to understand a great deal more about the human organism than just its anatomy and physiology, but also what underlies human suffering, what we were meant to become, and how estranged we find ourselves from our intended purpose.

LR: You know, the Sanskrit word for illness has more a meaning of imbalance, and encompasses not only the bodily pain and suffering, but also the everyday experiences which have produced discord and disharmony—disharmony not only in the body, but also in the mental functions and perceptions. The causes for many of these imbalances can be environmental and physical, but they can also be psychological, even spiritual. For instance, physical causal factors include such things as behavior, diet, seasonal extremes. But illnesses also come from psychological factors—whether one perceives and interacts with the world in a friendly or hostile way. And a spiritual illness would depend upon whether or not one derives purpose or meaning in his existence.

KC: So that an illness may awaken us to a painful awareness of the root of our illness—where in life we have fallen short.

LR: One could say that the root cause is the enormous *clinging* and *neediness* of all human beings. By "neediness" we mean seeing everything, whether outside ourselves or within, as an object which exists to fulfill our needs, demands, and pleasures.

KC: We see ourselves as separate from everything else—the center of our own universe—and our beliefs and deeply entrenched opinions orbit tightly around this self-made picture.

LR: That's right, and then every decision you make in your daily life is based on whether a person or event makes you happy or not, meets your needs. So those whom you feel meet your needs, you cling onto desperately, and those who do not, you deny and push them away. There is this dynamic going on, between aggression and a passionate clinging, and these set off the "energetic" imbalances. An enormous state of confusion is created, which clouds the mind, so that the psychic energies begin to affect the subtle physical energies, and you begin to get what we call psychosomatic symptoms—those related to body and mind together.

KC: Yes, and I get the sense that although someone comes to me with a pain in her chest, that behind this, it is her meaningless occupation, the inescapable economic difficulties which keep crying out. One gets the sense that as physicians we are treating the "pestilence" of the late twentieth century: Mankind, inextricably bound in a tangle of life's never-ending difficulties, has neither the personal wherewithal to face them or anywhere to fall except into some physical malady.

LR: Tibetans see symptoms as a symbol for where you are in this stage of your life, how you view the world. It may be the symptom is asking you to listen to your inner self, asking you to attend or be aware of the different processes or experiences that are going on. Then a headache becomes not merely a physiological pain, but something representing the intense agitation of your life—some kind of inner constriction.

140

KC: And then if we were to try to understand a movement toward wellness, it might be in studying our inner milieu, seeing the ways we are caught up by these tiny agitations and constrictions.

LR: Everything has to be in balance, not only the mind, body, and spirit, but the principal three energetic processes of a human being—the degrees of aggression, passion (or desire), and ignorance. Your health becomes more sound and vigorous when your life is not purely dictated by one of them, when you don't see the world from just one point of view. So we begin to see that spiritual practice—the inner work of awareness—relates to medical practice.

KC: In ancient cultures, the shaman or healer played an enormous role in the community's affairs—he was their priest, their wise man, their judge. He understood that the people in the village were under powerful and oftentimes conflicting forces and influences, and that an illness or epidemic might well represent an upset in the balance of these energies. There was the health of an individual to think of, as well as the health of the group as a whole, and these were intimately and inextricably related. The forces and laws that affected a single individual's health were the same that affected the tribe, and the same that were involved in environmental and climatic conditions, rainfall, water supply, the web of food chains, and so on. The doctor's concern was not only in eradicating a particular ache or pain, but of mediating between this great interplay of forces, and of tending the different aspects of each being—their bodies, of course, but also that which was beneath their bodies, that which was more essential and imperishable—call it their soul, or spirit, or whatever. I mention this because the picture I get of myself and my colleagues is a far cry from that noble vision. What do you look for in a true healer?

LR: In the Tibetan tradition, there are four categories of practitioners. The first, the Tibetan physician, requires seven years of training in a medical school, and becomes certified in the practice of traditional Tibetan medicine. And then there are psychic healers who use their own mental force or power to correct an illness (often going into trances or altered states of consciousness) and there are the faith healers, who act as channels or conduits for healing. And the last and most important in many ways is the *Rinpoche*, the highly spiritually evolved person, who through meditative and other practices has attained sufficient internal realization to intervene in the healing process. All four types of healers are sought in Tibet, but it is the *Rinpoche* who evaluates the entire clinical problem and helps decide what would be most useful.

KC: You might say that the *Rinpoche* embodies the most fundamental attributes of a great healer, one who can deeply see and feel what a patient needs, whether physical, psychological, or related to inner development.

LR: The Tibetan medical texts elaborate the essential qualities of a healer, the "perfections." The first and most important is compassion—not merely empathy, but the ability to feel the other person's pain within oneself, so much so that one becomes personally committed to the process of healing. There are other essential qualities of a practitioner, generosity, patience, perseverance, etc; but the other main one is the capacity never to turn patients away, whether or not they have resources, whether or not their personality is too intolerable or the demands on one's time too extreme.

KC: Yes, it is strange how much the situation has changed over the century. Today, Western doctors are oftentimes seen as highly educated, extraordinarily skilled technicians, able to ply our trade much like an excellent worker on an assembly line would build an expensive automobile. Yet how many of the qualities you mention do we embody? Around the turn of the century, there wasn't a great deal a doctor could do about most of the illnesses he faced, but at least he had time to attend his patients—to sit down at the bedside, take hold of a hand, worry over them. And never for a minute was his value doubted. Now we know and can do a great deal—and have so little time—something must have been forgotten. Do you think it is possible to reconcile this dilemma, to bring together the best of scientific progress with that which has been lost from former times?

LR: For many years now the Tibetans themselves have used a combination of Western medicine and traditional Tibetan medicine, with the lama or *Rinpoche* helping to choose which combination would be most appropriate. At times Western techniques are needed—the setting of a bone, surgical correction of appendicitis—but when there is a problem that requires an inner structuring, an inner balance, one in which the person's inner development is at stake, then I think Tibetan medicine is very relevant to the West.

KC: I agree, and yet we have to acknowledge the problems we face bringing the many forms of ancient and alternative medicine into the modern era, without watering them down so much that they become a fantasy, yet another kind of self-suggestion, or worse, chicanery. Most patients here expect to receive penicillin for a strep throat, expect to have an obstructed artery in their heart opened. Even though many are uncomfortable with the attention they are getting from their physicians of today—they know they aren't really being heard and that their deepest problems aren't really being touched— nonetheless, most people don't trust anything else either. And if they do, there is good possibility they will run into some form of alternative care which has little substance, little of the ancient wisdom Tibetan medicine has behind it. And to complicate matters further, we here in the West are simply a different people from someone living in Dharamsala or Mongolia. Not only is our conception of how things are and work in the world completely different, but so are our physical capacities, dietary habits, the stories we have been raised on, our religious and spiritual backgrounds. There are going to be difficulties bringing the great traditional knowledge and techniques of healing to a people and time so alien to these practices—to a Western mind unprepared and frequently unreceptive to such practices.

Let me ask you what has been the source of the great medical knowledge—those essential aspects of the healing arts, which span all epochs and cultures. I have heard it said that it was the Buddha who introduced many of the precepts of Tibetan medicine, and yet so many of the details must have come from centuries of careful, scientifically empirical study on the effects of herbs, dietary changes, variations in the weather and seasons, and so forth—factors so prominent in the ancient healing sciences. Could we say that both revelation and scientific empiricism stand behind the most authentic forms of medical knowledge?

LR: Yes, the Buddha did bring many of our medical practices, and these were passed down, but later the empirical approaches of Greek, Persian, Chinese and Indian medicine were amalgamated in. Seventy percent of Tibetan medicine comes from Indian, Ayurvedic medicine, which is based on the principle of observation. Part of Tibetan medicine has been passed down entirely through the oral tradition—never written down—and the other part is highly documented, with hundreds upon hundreds of different texts and literature.

KC: And what has been said of the real purpose of medical practice? I am reminded of the alchemists of the Middle Ages, whose work with gems and metals, and with medicine, simply assisted their greater work of transmutation—the study of their own evolution and transformation. Under those conditions the practice of medicine served as a basis of an inward inquiry of one's own meaning and inner possibilities, as well as an outward-directed work in caring for another person. The work of a physician was a work to fulfill one's obligation as a human being. If it is true that man was built to give, and that we have lost touch with this innate faculty, what better place could there be to search for it than in the practice of medicine?

LR: Let me put into context the purpose for taking up medicine for the traditional Tibetan physician. The Tibetan texts clearly state that a physician's calling offers an ideal opportunity to use the mundane life to work towards liberation, and that is because healing or being a physician provides the very basis of a good spiritual practice— the only profession that does so. So medicine is never merely a profession; it is a process of growth and inner development. The Buddhists speak of several paths leading in this direction—for example, the development of wisdom, compassion, concentration, perseverance, etc. And the practice of a physician provides a way to work on each of these. For example, the traditional healer must persevere to obtain the herbs he uses; he has to go into the mountains in his spare time to collect them. This takes perseverance.

KC: And that becomes a work of self-inquiry, does it not? At the same time we see how easily we are diverted, how quickly our interest is taken by our own personal problems—these human difficulties expose us to a tremendous vulnerability.

We also have to ask what it means to "help" our patients. A question like this cannot even be approached if we do not consider the entire range of human possibility. We can fix a bone, remove a wart, but then leave the deeper strata of a person totally without care. If an illness is nothing less than a measuring device, plumbing the depths of an individual's being, then what degree of harm as well as good are we doing making an incision only in the most superficial layers? The way to health is as unfathomable as the fundamental laws governing all of universal creation and destruction—and yet we are called to know something of both. I was taught from the beginning of medical school the Hippocratic aphorism *"primum non nocere"*—"first do no harm"; but firstly, are we sensitive enough to discriminate the needs of the spirit from those of the mortal body? To the degree that an illness stands as a person's story, we have to ask whether we have sufficient wisdom to edit that story.

LR: We have to be able to trust our inspiration, our vision of what is necessary in such moments, and our motivation toward searching for what is best for the patient. We need to keep open the question of whether we are obstructing the patient's inner growth process in some way while we are tending his bodily ailments. We are always coming to a very critical point of human experience, which is that of fundamental human suffering, and no matter how many ways one looks at it, as long as we are fragmented within ourselves, we inevitably will face a risk in making a choice—and courage is needed there.

KC: In trying to understand the essential elements of healing, we come back to Hippocrates, the great Greek physician of two thousand years age—really the grandparent of both ancient and modern medicine. To Hippocrates, everything in the cosmos was alive and intelligent, a continual movement of creation and destruction—a constant "exchange" of substances, upwards and downwards, as he put it—and it was the physician's task to mediate between these two great vertical movements. The same laws and processes, the same intelligence, which governed the cosmos regulated the workings of living nature, and Hippocrates saw in the human body that very same *intrinsic wisdom*—the innate capacity to heal itself. I am wondering how Tibetan medicine views this "wisdom of the body".

LR: I agree that the intrinsic nature of the body is self-regulating. Both the body and mind have this way of balancing themselves. Just as the sun comes out in the day and the moon at night—these two have a natural way of relating to each other—so, too, the body's energetic principles have the capacity of regulating and readjusting. But the human ego, or mind, is such that it cannot trust the process; it intervenes and ends up contributing to the process of disharmony and discord.

KC: So we are searching for an *inner orientation*, a more relaxed orientation, to allow this natural wisdom to act. Taken one step further, if it is true that all healing inevitably comes from "on high"—by "divine permission," as Avicenna, the great Sufi physician, has said— can we not consider our role as physicians that of helping to sound a call for this healing energy to penetrate this disordered state?

LR: The notion of divine or of a creator is not part of Buddhism. As we have said, we think of health and illness as related to an individual's own internal, unresolved issues, his own store of karma—this is the principal determinant of how our life or health will flow. Therefore, the fundamental process toward health is one towards enlightenment or liberation—liberation from the trappings of all the unconscious karmic factors stored in the mind, the ego's sense of self-worth.

KC: Perhaps you and I see this from slightly different angles, but then one doesn't necessarily have to posit a creator. That which is "higher," more divine or sacred, becomes that which helps us to turn inward, toward our natural Self—helps us to see our time-worn conditionings, the distractions and tenseness, which block the healing possibilities.

LR: Yes, and though we don't speak of an energy as being "higher," there is in Tibetan Buddhist practice what is called a *Siddhi*, a power-

146

ful force or energy which may act in the service of either spiritual development or health. And through your own attunement you can connect with this natural energy. Everyone experiences such extraordinary capacities at one time or another, so that we can begin to help our patients to identify these faculties in themselves.

KC: Doesn't something have to be given up or sacrificed to assist this process? Our everyday self wants to grasp feverishly onto health, but our more interior, more essential, faculties need to open to it in a less acquisitive way. Agreed, the idea of sacrifice takes on such a loaded or pejorative meaning today, but in the ancient ceremonies and rituals of thousands of years ago, might not the medicine men have known of a more authentic kind of sacrifice? My question is in the direction of what may have been the original meaning of sacrifice, of "making sacred"—of "*making available,*" making a place for this reconciling energy to act. Rather than remaining a repository for all of life's ills, cannot the body be directed toward its more rightful function, that of containing and circulating the healing waters of awareness?

LR: A great deal has to be let go of—old patterns, aspects of lifestyle. When you let go of your needs, you connect back to the natural state of the self-regulating mechanisms of the mind and body. I also see sacrifice as a way of connecting with the sacred—in the sense of an *offering*. When you put yourself up on the stage of life and open yourself up to it, make yourself vulnerable, you are making an offering, and you are more likely then to connect to the sacred nature of your being—the pristine clarity of the Mind which contains the harmonious, natural self-regulating processes.

KC: As doctors, we always need to come back to this same offering, do we not?

LR: In almost all sessions with a patient we are provided the opportunity to offer ourselves to the client, in a very open, sharing, and vulnerable way—then a sacred space is created between us and the client.

KC: This may seem overly idealistic, but for a long time now I have gotten the sense that I help my patients less through scientific know-how and more through spending a little time to chat and listen to them, returning to the old ways, so to speak. We both need this time—to step back from our "performance" as patient and doctor—to allow this sacred connection you are speaking of to appear.

LR: It is very special—one can feel a terrible sense of emptiness then, but at the same time a deeper, profound yearning may well up, a longing for something which is sacred. It is a yearning that is very intangible, for something that can never be possessed.

KC: At that moment one feels more alive. It can then become another driving force in life, an innate, vital force. In that moment we know how helpless and inadequate we are to the task—we are tasting human suffering and, as physicians, taking part of it onto ourselves, and this is an entirely new level of encounter.

LR: Absolutely, we are talking about the eternal dilemma of the human experience. And this takes a kind of courage and strength, to take in and embrace all this pain, discomfort, and suffering of another. As a physician, when I recognize that I am totally helpless, unsure of what to do, and yet have the courage to experience that helplessness and uncertainty, I think this becomes an essential part of the healing process. This is what allows the client to feel a deeply human connection with the physician, a heart-to-heart connection, a sort of bonding through sharing, and this brings an important *trust* to the relationship. And there is another kind of trust that is necessary—the capacity of the patient, in spite of all the paranoia, demandingness, neediness, to accept that the physician doesn't have all the answers—that both are engaged in a part of life where nobody really has the full answer. This is where trust becomes an important component.

KC: Yes, one doesn't want to put oneself is the position of being an "authoritarian," but our patients would like there to be someone with a sense of genuine authority; someone in whom the patient can place trust, but who is not domineering, and this takes an unusual sincerity on the part of the healer. On one hand we are looking for a nurturing, "feminine," quality, the taking on of everything the patient needs to release, and on the other, a very "masculine" tenacity is required to stand in the eye of the storm of the patient's negativities and vulnerabilities.

LR: A warm quality of presence, I feel, is very necessary—not just a caring attitude, or worse, one that is put-on, in terms of verbalizing concern and so forth, but if there is a real presence and sense of spaciousness, the patient can feel that whatever he or she says, you are able to contain it. This spaciousness of mind is the natural state of the mind, it is the essence of Buddhist practice. There needs to be this warmth and presence, and, in addition, a *clarity*—not only clarity in being able to understand what the client is saying, but manifesting a clarity in one's presence—a spaciousness and capacity to receive.

KC: We are often closer to such moments when a disease process reaches its most critical stage. In former centuries, something very essential was understood about the period of "crisis"—this time of confrontation between the tendency toward illness and the tendency toward health. Franz Mesmer—apparently a remarkable healer, but so unconventional he was totally ostracized by his colleagues—spoke of it as a moment of possibility, when patient and physician reached a "rapport or covenant"—a clearer vision into the workings of the illness and the direction to be taken toward recovery.

LR: I, too, believe that the crisis provides a more shared experience of the human condition; it brings the healer into the realm of the patient's world, so that the healer suddenly realizes his own and the other's vulnerability, opens to these, to the possibility of a more moving, human interaction, a more essential or genuine empathy.

KC: We are speaking of energies and movements which are extraordinarily subtle. Surely these most imperceptible levels of human existence can only be perceived by an entirely different scale of sensitivity and attentiveness. If we are to understand the confluence of forces determining an individual's health, are we not going to have to "look" with a different, more sensitive part of the mind? What level of observation are we being called to?

LR: It depends upon which *level* the physician, and the physician's perception are operating. When we work at the level of technology, medicine as a trade, then healing is a process of learned practice, and you end up following defined guidelines and practice on that basis. I think, though, that there are physicians who go beyond this, and enter into another level of experience. Then there is a respect for the immediacy of whatever is going on between the two, and in such encounters there may be a sudden spontaneous vision which helps clarify the situation. Again, this is what we mean when the experience becomes more transcendental, more collective, a more sacred experience—the medical procedure is taken into a sacred state.

KC: And this quality of "sacred medicine" takes the sum total of our willingness to face our own life, our own frailties. We are amidst great forces and difficulties at this moment and we must stay with the struggle and not turn from it.

LR: Then there is a moment in the process where the patient is completely empty; all the anger and pent-up negativities are released, and there is nothing left but a much deeper sadness and openness. And being able to find that state is very important from a Buddhist point of view. Whereas in the West, we identify such moments with psychological instability, even psychosis, if one can find the spaciousness to contain all of this, there is a resurgence of energy which can be very helpful. But all this takes patience and perseverance, and the ability to trust the process. Then we are connecting back to the naturalness of the psyche.

KC: I want to change direction slightly and ask about the place of the physical body. How is it that we have forgotten that, while the purpose of medicine is to mend the body, it is also to help it toward its rightful role, that of a servant to something higher in the destiny of *Homo sapiens*. On one hand, we spend much of our time overly concerned about our bodies and our health, trapped in a round of innumerable hypochondriacal symptoms. Yet, one gets the sense that we seldom pay the right kind of attention to our bodies—we indulge our appetites and aches almost as a ritual. We don't live our lives; our bodies demand to live them for us. And when we look back on the more ancient forms of medicine, whether Chinese, Ayurvedic, or whatever, each seems to begin with basic principles of knowing precisely what the physical body requires. I recently picked up the Jewish philosopher and physician Moses Maimonides' *Treatise on Health*, and he begins with a fundamental dictum—which he attributes to the lineage of Hippocrates—that "the preservation of health lies in abstaining from satiation and avoidance of excessive exertion." How simple and primary—that we simply need to take care to understand what the body requires, without letting it take over, without overindulging it.

LR: We might take that idea further from the point of view of the complex relationship between mind and body. On one hand, seen from the ordinary, cognitive level of Buddhism, healing the body is merely seen as a service to the mind—the metaphor often being used of the body being the "horse'" on which its master, the mind, rides. And then a physical illness is seen as a reflection of one's state of mind. Now, in the more sophisticated, higher forms of tantric Buddhism, the mind and body are equally interdependent, one as part of the other. One way to look at this is the mind being the embodiment of the feminine principle, and the body an embodiment of the masculine principle; and just as a family cannot exist without the man and woman conjoining, similarly, the individual cannot remain healthy without the mind and body correctly interacting. The mind is constantly giving cues to the body and vice versa. Thus, we encourage a patient to enter into meditative experiences as an educative process to understand what the body is like—to see the relationship between mind and body.

KC: So if we are aiming for physical health—seeing that in its present state, the body lacks the aptitude to maintain itself—we can begin by turning an active awareness toward the body, developing a "cooperative relationship" between our mind and body. We might then become more sensibly, rather than hypochondriacally, aware of the interior energies.

LR: Being aware of the body even when we are in a healthy state would be very helpful, rather than just when we are sick.

KC: One might liken the body to a laboratory—our own laboratory—and if we can begin to study the movements, energies, and laws transacting within it, we have a possibility of understanding the processes that produce ill health.

LR: For instance, if you practice this awareness during and after a meal, you suddenly begin to notice you are overeating slightly; you become attentive to a greater-than-normal fullness in the stomach.

KC: One begins to understand some of the great tenets of Eastern medicine, such as we should eat until the stomach is no more than three-quarters full—one begins to verify for oneself some of the great teachings.

Again, to move on: you can't be in the practice of medicine for very long without being touched with the intensity of the suffering and discomfort everywhere. I don't mean that everyone we see is suffering the ravages of some terminal illness, but I do get the feeling that everybody is being dragged under by the weight of their own personal difficulties, or at least by their attitude toward them. I have been talking with many of my students about this, and there seems to be an unwritten, yet universal, precept, implanted very insidiously in every medical student: the certainty that, as a doctor, "you can't allow yourself to become too 'involved' with your patients"—you can't allow their pain and suffering to overwhelm you, or, as it is said, "it will tear you apart." You have to remain clinical—insulated and detached. So many of us doctors seem then to forget the very reason we went into medicine; in the aftermath of the Scientific Revolution, we seem to have kept our heads but lost our hearts. And then I turn to a tradition such as Tibetan medicine, and I see a central thread running through the entire teaching, the idea of the universality of human suffering, and the need to find a strength and compassion—not some diluted, sophomoric sentimentality—but a genuine willingness to embrace the immense magnitude of human discomfort. We are seeing suffering as part of every life —integral, in a way, to all of universal workings—but we need to discriminate between a suffering which leads us toward healing and one that is merely "egoistic," and that wears the body down.

LR: Buddhists view suffering as an elemental process of life, something that pervades virtually every experience. For instance, even if I feel very cold and then go out into the sun, that becomes a source of warmth, comfort, and happiness for me, but at the same time I begin to worry if it will last, or I am already creating the cause for sunburn—so that every happiness or comfort has a source of discomfort and suffering imbedded within it. And although we understand this with our minds, our emotional life cannot really figure it out. The way Buddhist physicians approach a suffering patient, therefore, is first to create a tolerable comfort zone, and then begin to address the nature of suffering, without this appearing defeating or punishing to the patient. We all have to understand that underlying every form of human experience, there is the potential for suffering. And from the Buddhist perspective, this is not taken negatively or with a sense of despair—you don't allow it to overwhelm you. It is just another experience of the psyche, and we can develop the capacity to see such experiences with a quality of detachment.

KC: Suffering, then, has the possible nature of becoming transformative—if it is taken as an experience, and is not totally engulfing. We need to remember that illness and suffering are part and parcel of being born, and they may jolt us into asking why we were born. But even more, we need to come back to how tightly caught all of us are in our own daily sufferings. How are we, as physicians, to feel the pain and suffering of another, when much of the time we are lost in our own protective fears and discomforts? I cannot help, if my concern is a lie, a subterfuge. Much of the time I am entangled between a movement toward caring, and one that doesn't give a damn for the other person—and that is painful.

LR: But to be aware that I don't care or don't know what to do is itself a quality of compassion.

KC: We keep returning to the centrality of our mental processes in healing, and I know when you speak of the mind, you are doing so from a far different perspective than I was taught in medical school. We all know of the nearly irreparable rent which appeared some 400 years ago in the Western world between what we call mind and the physical universe—between the mind and body. Modern science seems to have kept the "baby," the physical body, and discarded the mind as some dirty bathwater—we have reduced the mind to inanimate, physical and chemical processes, a mere effluent spilling out from the brain like some industrial pollutant. And yet we keep hearing of the need for a cooperative link between these two "incommensurable" entities.

LR: Yes, you are implying that the Buddhist definition of the mind is very different from the Western. For the Buddhist, the mind is a state of awareness, the ability to perceive or be aware of whatever it is experiencing—itself, as well as objects external to itself. In addition, we define mind as being innately a state of clarity, like a mirror. And this is important to understand when we are connecting this important theme to healing, since we are not merely interested in uncovering negative feelings or old patterns of behavior—we are not simply interested in psychological analysis—but in having the patient appreciate this "innate nature of the mind." Helping a person relate to the spacious, expansive nature of the mind helps him connect to a very fundamental process in himself. The mind then becomes an unbiased, unprejudiced reflecting agent, totally nonjudgmental, and you begin to approach your life and illness with that attitude. For example, you see anxiety as just another experience in the vast expanse of the psyche, merely being hosted by consciousness—appearing, lasting for a duration, then dissolving back into its own base, the mind.

KC: Once again we come back to the ageless law of impermanence—of everything in continual movement, perpetual creation and dissolution—birth and death. We are beginning to explore the workings of the mind.

LR: The natural mind has the capacity on its own to let painful thoughts or physical experiences come up, and then dissolve. It is like a flower growing—you let it be, it grows into beauty, and then dies. The same with many of our mental and physical experiences. However, our ego interferes with this natural rhythm; our mind won't let anything be just what it is, won't allow the very basic state of awareness which has the potential for clarity.

KC: When there is a softening, a more accepting attitude, toward our experiences, we begin to feel more whole—more vital and healthy—at least for the briefest moment, do we not?

LR: I think that when you see your mental and physical experiences from a more neutral state, you are respecting a part of yourself which you know little about, and then you are giving it a reality and "tangibility." You begin trusting the natural rhythm of the psyche and the body, and begin to sense these with a sense of freshness, without preconceptions. If I say, "Oh, my body always gets tired in the afternoon," that preconception then dictates how I feel in the afternoon. But if I impartially experience the cold weather giving me a headache, and the hot producing indigestion, then I'm not imposing my opinions and preconceptions onto my body.

Of course, we have to remember that there are many levels of this mind: from the coarse, purely sensory and conceptual level, to the very subtle state of mind which is pure energy.

KC: And, as mentioned, these different levels of mind go hand in hand with different gradations of our ability to perceive our being, and different levels of connection to the healing process.

LR: Absolutely! At the first level, you totally believe in what you see and what you feel, and get stuck there, whereas in the finer levels, where the essence of the mind and body are pure energy, the two become indistinguishable, and you begin to have a sense of harmony or interplay of the two.

KC: Then we are seeing a relationship between the mind and body which is not just a clever, 1960s slogan, but a palpable relationship, a real connection, between the movements and energies of the body and those of the mind. And we are experiencing our own life; our own energy, relating these two.

Inevitably, we have to turn to the role of healer in leading a patient toward death, a death worthy of life itself. Here again, Western medicine sees this experience in very concrete terms—the light, whatever that is, simply goes out, the chemical reactions cease, the structural proteins and carbohydrates gradually disassemble themselves back into primal particles. Oblivion! Whatever else there is remains unfathomable or in the realm of religion, and not subject to valid scientific interrogation. Death has become our opponent, a naked failure on the part of medical science. And yet, surely we are not relegated to fighting every death, or simply assuaging the fearful grip death holds on all of us?

LR: In Tibetan medicine, there is always the effort on the part of the physician to maintain life as long as possible, but once the lama determines that the death signs have passed beyond a certain, irreversible stage, there is the strong belief that it is better not to interfere with the dying process. It is also important to remember that when we think about death, Tibetan Buddhists think about it as death of the physical body, because there is a very subtle part of the mental and physical energies which "continue" into another level of existence. But most important to understand is that physical death provides an opportunity for inner growth; it is one of those times where a great clarity of mind dawns, which can be used by the patient for his or her own evolution. Even the youngest children in Tibet understand life and death from this point of view, that death is approached as another part of the evolutionary process, and although there is, of course, grieving at the time of someone's death, everyone understands that this is another experience of the eternal interplay of the human condition. It can be approached with clinging, neediness, an overwhelming sense of despair, or as a natural part of the evolutionary process, and this choice is up to each one of us and to every family as well.

KC: That's very helpful—seeing the dying process as an opportunity, a study. But accepting one's inevitable death must be an act far greater than mere resignation, or thinly disguised imagining. Isn't it our first and last clinging to our own living existence?

LR: Yes, that is true, and the issue is not just death, but the aging processes as well. I mean there is an overwhelming distaste for aging, which is a precursor to death, and without addressing the two, the dying process becomes one of mere hopelessness. You know, many people prefer being sick to aging. People don't mind breaking their leg as long as they don't develop wrinkles. They would rather dwell on their illness than accept their aging.

KC: We are living in a culture that has been educated poorly. We haven't been told that what happens in death is exactly what happens every day in life, that the whole of life can be seen as a preparation for our death. So maybe our mistake is that we wait until death to face death.

LR: I think a very practical idea would be to set aside a day two or three times a year—as we do in Tibet—where you meditate, or go into a workshop or retreat, where you consider the impermanence and changing nature of life. Not only thinking about these questions, but actually, while meditating or sitting quietly, feeling oneself going through constant change, physically, emotionally and so forth.

KC: Experiences like these need not be depressing. They connect us to this universal search, which has taken place in mankind throughout the millennia.

Healing in Ancient Egypt

LISE MANNICHE

In Ancient Egypt health and equilibrium were thought to be related to the divine and cosmic, as well as the earthly, spheres.[1.] To ordinary mortals, health meant more than simply not being ill, and the process of obtaining physical well-being and conquering disease is the subject of most of the surviving texts of pharaonic date. The body needed to be "complete" not only in this life, but, in order to fulfil its functions in eternity, beyond the grave as well. To ensure this "whole" appearance, the Egyptians developed the art of embalming, as exhibited in images of the human body in Egyptian funerary art.

While on earth, the ideal of health was thought to be a happy heart, flourishing limbs, a neck sitting firm under the head, eyes looking into the distance, a nose breathing and drawing in air, ears standing open and hearing, mouth opened and knowing how to make an answer, arms flourishing and capable of working.[2] The healthy human should be able to eat, drink, copulate, and evacuate the bowels. Such a person would be "like someone with old age yet ahead, who sleeps until dawn, free from suffering, without cough." A state of perpetual youth was not necessarily the sole aim, for the texts often speak of attaining old age, the ideal span being 110 years. But old age is qualified by the word *nfr* ("beautiful" in the broadest sense of the word,

158

corresponding perhaps to Arabic *hasan*). This rather suggests that physical health alone was not all.

The Egyptians gave the world a comprehensive pharmacopoeia to help cure diseases. Medical papyri written around 1500 B.C., but dating back perhaps another thousand years, abound in prescriptions. The formula was as follows: "If you [the practitioner] examine a patient who suffers from [followed by a detailed description of the symptoms], then you shall say: This is [identification of the disease]. This is a case that I will treat/I will fight [here follows the treatment]." But some cases were untreatable, either because they were hopeless, or because the illness would take its own course. In the latter case, the patient was told to rest in bed until the affliction had passed.

The Egyptians had written treatises on "the vessels" (this term including veins and arteries, as well as sinews) connecting various parts of the body, and there is evidence of their understanding the humors, a fundamental concept of Hippocratic and later Arabic tradition.[3] Yet in most cases it is the individual symptoms which command the attention of the practitioner. It was not his task to treat "the whole person."

Apart from accidental injuries, disease was attributed to several factors. Herodotus, the Greek historian who is such a mine of information on life in Egypt in the 5th century B.C., was told that the Egyptians of his day believed all sickness to be caused by the food they ate (a theory reflected in traditional Arab medicine); corrective measures were taken by fasting for three consecutive days every month.[4] In pharaonic times disease was primarily thought to be caused by putrefaction of food residue. But, in addition to man's own responsibility, dead persons, gods, or demons had the power to single out an individual and cause suffering as a means of revenge. "The one whom god loves, him he shall keep alive," reads the introduction to one of the medical texts, which is otherwise more concerned with sickness than with health.

As in our day, physicians concentrated on their special fields and would tackle the individual symptoms of the patient, no doubt successfully in a great many instances. The fame of Egyptian physicians reached far beyond the borders of the country: The Persian kings of Egypt in the 6th century B.C. relied solely on Egyptian physicians. But the sick had other options than swallowing pills and potions and applying bandages.

The medical men were closely connected with the temples of learning and knowledge. The House of Life was where scribes were trained and where papyrus scrolls which formed the basis of their knowledge were stored. The duties of members of the clergy would overlap with those of the physician. There is reference to an "overseer of priests of the goddess Sakhmet, overseer of magicians, the king's chief physician who reads the book daily, who treats anyone who is ill, who lays his hand on the patient, getting to know him." The physician used his hand to test the patient's pulse and the temperature and texture of the skin. This, however, was to assist him in diagnosis rather than treatment. A priest reported himself "skillful in judging illness...my magic applies to the sick face, my spells to the [bad] odor."

Whereas the medical texts describe the patient's body as the object of the practitioner's ministrations, the temple offered a treatment which required the patient's mind to be fully present as well. People came to the temple seeking healing from the resident deity and slept in a sanatorium adjoining the temple, where the deity would visit them in their dreams.[5] They bathed in water which had touched the statue of the god or goddess, and they had facilities for meditation. It was a well-known fact that the psychological frame of mind of the patient had a bearing on his health and on the outcome of any treatment, and incubation in the proximity of the deity would assist in the healing process.

The sacred and the profane united in the use of scent. Recipes were so important that they were inscribed in stone on the walls of the temples. The most legendary scent from Egypt was *kyphi*, which can be traced at least as far back as the 16th century B.C. It was used in fumigation as well as being taken internally, and it served the multiple purposes of aiding communication with the god, uplifting the spirit, and curing ailments. No one has described it better than Plutarch: "Without drunkenness it relaxes and loosens the chain-like sorrows and tensions of daily cares. It polishes and purifies like a mirror the faculty which is imagination and receptive to dreams, like the notes of the lyre which the Pythagoreans used before sleep, to charm and heal the emotive and irrational or the soul. For odors often recall the power of perception when it is failing, while often they obscure and calm it since the exhalations penetrate through the body by reason of their smooth softness."[6] Although this was written in the beginning of the second century A.D. based on a treatise written some 400 years earlier (now lost), it reflects the fact that the ancient Egyptians had long been aware that scent has a therapeutic effect. Although the ingredients of *kyphi* were recorded, its preparation was shrouded in secrecy. It continued to be made for centuries.

An unguent maker of the Middle Ages revealed that while the ingredients were ground, the seven Greek vowels were to be recited. In view of the fact that Hellenistic tradition assigned a vowel to each of the spheres of the universe, thus achieving perfect harmony, are we to imply that *kyphi* absorbed similar cosmic properties and produced harmony in the soul?

That the image of a god possessed healing powers is demonstrated by the fact that in the reign of Rameses II (c. 1100 B.C.) a statue of the god Khonsu was sent from Egypt to the distant land of Bakhtan to heal a princess possessed by an evil spirit when conventional medicine, also administered by an Egyptian, had failed. Khonsu, originally a moon god, had a following as healer and protector to pious Egyptians. To remove his sacred image from the temple was an extraordinary gesture on behalf of the king.

The art of healing is personified in the ibis-headed god Thoth, who was also lord of writing and magic. In the realm of mythology we witness the contest of the "two divine brothers" Horus and Seth concerning the rulership of the world. They came to blows and Horus tore off his brother's testicles, while Seth extracted the eye of Horus. In popular belief Horus emerged as the hero, while Seth remained the villain. By being the one who healed and restored the eye, Thoth became the great healer, and the eye was seen as the symbol of health, an amulet of universal significance.

Horus appeared as the injured party in another myth, namely as a child wandering in the marshes of the Delta. When a scorpion stung him, with near fatal consequences, his mother Isis came to the rescue with her knowledge of healing and magic. She became the great healing goddess of later antiquity, her cult spreading as far north as Britain. "The Egyptians say that Isis is the inventor of many remedies for health and that she has vast experience in medical science. That is why, having achieved immortality, she dedicated herself to treating human beings and, during sleep, she gives assistance to those who ask, and manifests herself clearly and reveals her benevolence to those in need.... During sleep, in fact, while keeping close she gives help for sickness, and those who serve her are healed against all expectations. Many who were given up by the doctors because of the severity of their illness have been served by her. People deprived of sight, or the use of some member, have been restored to normal after having taken refuge with the goddess."[7]

If it was within the power of the Egyptian pantheon to heal, this was a privilege extended posthumously to certain human beings. Most prominently Imhotep, an architect, magician, and wise man in the reign of King Zoser (ca. 2700 B.C.) near the end of the pharaonic period, was credited with medical skills, to the extent that he was eventually identified with Asclepios of the Greeks. A myth was created around Imhotep's person, and his tomb (as yet undiscovered) in the vicinity of Memphis south of Cairo provided the focal point for pilgrimages. His cult was established in other parts of Egypt, where his healing was sought not only in the temple through incubation, dreams, and oracles, but also by people at home through prayer.

NOTES

1. On Ancient Egyptian healing and medicine among others: S.Sigerist, A *History of Medicine*, vol. I (New York: 1987); H. v. Deines and H. Grapow, *Grundriss der Medizin der alten Agypter*, vol. 3, *Kranker, Krankheiten und Artz*, (Berlin: 1956); "Medicine" in *The Legacy of Egypt*, ed J.R. Harris, (Oxford: Clarendon Press, 1971); L. Manniche, *An Ancient Egyptian Herbal* (London: British Museum Press, and Austen: Texas University Press, 1989).

2. From a scribe's exercise book ca. 800 B.C.: A. Erman, *The Literature of the Ancient Egyptians* (London: 1927, 174).

3. On traditional Arab medicine see, among others: H.G.M. Chishti, *The Traditional Healer's Handbook* Vermont 1988, 1991; Ibn Qayyim, *The Medicine of the Prophet*, (Cambridge, England: The Islamic Texts Society).

4. Herodotus, II,77 (Loeb edition, 1946).

5. *Lexicon der Agyptologie,* ed. W. Helck and E. Otto (Wiesbaden: 1972), s.v. "Sanatorium."
6. *De Iside et Osiride* 80. transl. G. Griffiths, (University of Wales Press, 1970).
7. Diodorus Siculus, *Library of History,* I,25 (Loeb edition, 1968).

The Kung Approach to Healing

RICHARD KATZ

"Tell our story of healing to your people." The Kung people (some-times known as the Zhuntwasi or Bushmen) of the Kalahari Desert in Botswana, just north of South Africa, gave me that charge. Boiling Energy, which has been excerpted below, is one way I have tried to fulfill that charge. But their charge is a continually unfolding responsibility. Since Boiling Energy was published, much has changed—and fortunately much has survived. Though until recently still hunter-gatherers, the Kung are now pursued by the threat of losing their land, the source of their life. Yet their heal-ing dance remains, seeking new and more intense expressions. We have much to learn from the Kung. But today we must go beyond "learning from" toward a more concrete and reciprocal exchange. We must support the Kung struggle for their land or their healing tradition may be terminally uprooted.

—Richard Katz

For the Kung, healing is more than curing, more than the application of medicine. Healing seeks to establish health and growth on physi-cal, psychological, social, and spiritual levels; it involves work on the individual, the group, and the surrounding environment and cosmos.

164

Healing pervades Kung culture, as a fundamental integrating and enhancing force. The culture's emphasis on sharing and egalitarianism, its vital life of the spirit and strong community, are expressed in and supported by the healing tradition. The central event in this tradition is the all-night healing dance.

Four times a month on the average, night signals the start of a healing dance. The women sit around the fire, singing and rhythmically clapping. The men, sometimes joined by women, dance around the singers. As the dance intensifies, *num*, or spiritual energy, is activated in the healers, both men and women, but mostly among the dancing men. As *num* is activated in them, they begin to *kia*, or experience an enhancement of their consciousness. While experiencing *kia*, they heal all those at the dance. Before the sun rises fully the next morning, the dance usually ends. Those at the dance find it exciting, joyful, powerful.

The dance is a community event in which the entire camp participates. The people's belief in the healing power of *num* brings substance to the dance. All who come are given healing. In the dance, the people confront the uncertainties and contradictions of their experience, attempting to resolve issues dividing the group, reaffirming the group's spiritual cohesion. And they do so in a way which is harmonious with their own and their culture's maintenance and growth.

The Kung do not look upon their healing dances as separate from the other activities of daily life. Like hunting, gathering, and socializing, dancing is another thing they do. The dance is a point of marked intensity and significance in their lives.

Healing is not reserved for a few persons with unique characteristics or extraordinary powers. Nor is there a special class or caste or guild of healers, enjoying special privileges in the culture. By the time they reach adulthood, more than half the men and ten percent of the women have become healers.

These characteristics of the dance establish its importance in the study of healing and consciousness. Moreover, the dance seems to be an old part of Kung hunting-gathering life. The rock paintings of South Africa include depictions of a healing dance much like the *dwa*, or Giraffe, the dominant healing dance of today. The healing dance must therefore be at least several hundred years old, and perhaps older.

Many kinds of fundamental activities are focused in the dance. Healing in the most generic sense is provided. It may take the form of curing an ill body or mind, as the healer pulls out the sickness; or of mending the social fabric, as the dance provides for a manageable release of hostility and an increased sense of social solidarity; or of protecting the village from misfortune, as the healer pleads with the gods for relief from the Kalahari's harshness. And the healing takes the form of enhancing consciousness, as the dance brings its participants into contact with the spirits and gods.

The dance provides the training ground for aspiring healers. It also provides the healers with opportunities for fulfillment and growth, where all can experience a sense of well-being, and where some may experience what Westerners would call a spiritual development. In the dance, the Kung find a vehicle for artistic expression. And from the dance, they receive profound knowledge, as the healer reports on those extended encounters with the gods which can occur during especially difficult healing efforts.

These activities are integrated with and reinforce each other, forming a continuous source of curing, counsel, protection, and enhancement. The healing is stimulated by the atmosphere generated at the dance. As individual healers go into *kia*, other Kung participating in the dance in various ways and to various degrees themselves experience an alteration of their state of consciousness, even if they do not go into *kia*. An atmosphere develops in which one person's experience of *kia* has a contagious effect on others.

Certain events or happenings make a dance more likely to occur, such as a severe illness, especially if it is sudden; the killing of a big game animal; the return of absent family members; and visits from close relatives or "important" persons, like anthropologists. Most often dances are held because people want to sing and dance together, as part of their continuing effort to prevent incipient sickness, which they believe resides in everyone, from becoming severe and manifest; as part of their desire to contact the gods and seek their protection; as part of their wish to have an evening of enjoyment and companionship.

The actual frequency of dances is influenced by ecological and sociological factors, a most important one being whether the Kung are camped at a permanent water-hole or out in the bush. When they are camped around the permanent water-holes, though their hunting and gathering remain demanding, camps move infrequently and then only for short distances. This leaves more time and energy available for dances, which can occur once, perhaps twice a week. When the Kung are out in the bush, especially as the dry season approaches, they are constantly on the move, and their hunting, gathering, and water collection can require greater effort. Less time and energy are available for dancing. Dances occur perhaps two or three times a month, and then usually to treat a specific illness.

No special equipment is necessary for the dance. Dance rattles (*zhorosi*) are used when available. They are made from dried cocoons with pieces of ostrich eggshell inside, strung on pieces of fiber. Preferably, a pair of rattles is used, one string being wrapped around each of the dancer's calves, though when rattles are in short supply, a dancer may use only one string. Usually several pairs are available at the average-sized dance. As the dancers move around the circle, each step elicits the distinctive staccato sound of the rattles, which accompanies and accents the rhythmic texture of the dance. Most dancers also bring their walking stick to the dance. This stick, which can also be used for digging roots and carrying objects, is carved from a piece of stripped hardwood, usually with a large gnarled knot at the top serving as a handle. They use the stick to accent their dancing steps or, especially when fatigued, to support themselves as they continue to dance.

In their curing efforts, healers may use plant substances which contain *num*. These plants are ground to a powder, mixed with marrow or fat, and put in an empty tortoise shell, several inches long. Healers place a burning coal into the mixture, wafting the smoke, which carries *num*, toward the patient.

The Kung say that *kia* comes from the activation of an energy that they call *num*. *Num* was originally given to the Kung by the gods. Though experiencing *kia* is a necessary prerequisite to healing, it is painful and feared. The cause of *kia*—the activated *num*—is said to

167

boil fiercely within the person. Some at the dance avoid *kia;* others experience *kia* but fail to develop it so that it can be applied to healing. Even among the healers, not all heal at every dance.

Those who have learned to heal are said to "possess" *num.* They are called *num kausi,* "masters, or owners, of *num.*" *Num* resides in the pit of the stomach and the base of the spine. As healers continue their energetic dancing, becoming warm and sweating profusely, the *num* in them heats up and becomes a vapor. It rises up the spine to a point approximately at the base of the skull, at which time *kia* results. Kinachau, an old healer, talks about the *kia* experience: "You dance, dance, dance, dance. Then *num* lifts you up in your belly and lifts you in your back, and you start to shiver. *Num* makes you tremble; it's hot. Your eyes are open, but you don't look around; you hold your eyes still and look straight ahead. But when you get into *kia,* you're looking around because you see everything, because you see what's troubling everybody. Rapid shallow breathing draws *num* up. What I do in my upper body with the breathing, I also do in my legs with the dancing. You don't stomp harder, you just keep steady. Then *num* enters every part of your body, right to the tip of your feet and even your hair."

The action and ascent of *num* are described by Kau Dwa, another powerful healer: "In your backbone you feel a pointed something and it works its way up. The base of your spine is tingling, tingling, tingling, tingling. Then *num* makes your thoughts nothing in your head."

Num is an energy held in awe and considered very powerful and mysterious. This same energy is what the healer "puts into" people in attempting to cure them. For once heated up, *num* can both induce *kia* and combat illness.

As Kung learn to have some control over their boiling *num,* they can apply the *num* to healing. They learn to *twe,* that is, to "heal" or "pull out sickness," or simply "pull." Kau Dwa describes how one can heal while experiencing *kia:* "When you *kia,* you see things that you must pull out, like the death things that god has put into people. You see people properly, just as they are. Your vision does not whirl."

Kau Dwa is blind, and he describes the vision of *kia* as follows: "I was working hard at healing people, but people didn't pay me. I was working hard at putting things into their *gebesi* [internal organs], but people didn't pay me or give me things. So god collected my eyes and took them away. God keeps my eyeballs in a little cloth bag. When he first collected them, he got a little cloth bag and plucked my eyeballs out and put them into the bag, and then he tied the eyeballs to his belt and went up to heaven. And now when I dance, on the nights that I dance and when the singing rises up, god comes down from heaven swinging the bag with the eyeballs above my head, and he lowers the eyeballs to my eye level, and as the singing gets strong, he puts the eyeballs into my sockets and they stay there and I heal. And when the women stop singing and separate out, he removes the eyeballs, puts them back in the cloth bag, and takes them up to heaven."

During *kia*, the Kung experience themselves as existing beyond their ordinary level. As Kinachau puts it: "When we enter *kia*, we are different from when our *num* is not boiling and small. We can do different things."

Kia itself is an intense, emotional state. Emotions are aroused to an extraordinary level, whether they be fear or exhilaration or seriousness. The Kung also practice extraordinary activities during *kia*. They perform cures and, as part of their effort to heal, may handle and walk on fire, see the insides of people's bodies and scenes at great distances from their camp, or travel to god's home—activities never attempted in their ordinary state. Moreover, they experience themselves as beyond their ordinary selves by becoming more essential, more themselves. Toma Zho, perhaps the strongest healer at Xaixai, speaks of this increased essentiality: "I want to have a dance soon so that I can really become myself again."

According to Kau Dwa, you must die in *kia*. Trying to clarify his meaning, I asked him: "Does that mean really die?"

"Yes."

"I mean *really* die."

"Yes."

"You mean die like when you are buried beneath the ground?" I am already struggling with my words.

"Yes," Kau Dwa replies with enthusiasm. "Yes, just like that!"

"They are the same?"

"Yes, the same. It is death I speak of," he affirms.

"No difference?" I almost plead.

"It is death," he responds firmly but softly.

"The death where you never come back?" I am nearly at the end of my logical rope.

"Yes," he says simply, "it is that bad. It is the death that kills us all."

"But the healers get up, and a dead person doesn't." My statement trails off into a question.

"That is true," Kau Dwa replies quietly, with a smile, "healers may come alive again."

The education of men and women healers differs, but the differences are more matters of form and structure than process and experience. One of the most striking things about the Kung education for healing is that it is an aspect of normal socialization. Most males and more than a third of the women try to become healers. Long before persons seriously try to become healers, they play at entering *kia*. A group of five- and six-year-olds may perform a small "healing dance," imitating the actual dance, with its steps and healing postures, at times falling as if in *kia*. Through play, the children are modeling; as they grow up, they are learning about *kia*. Furthermore, education for healing occurs within the context of the family, the major vehicle for socialization. The primary source of information about *kia*, as well as the experiential teacher of *kia*, is likely to be in one's immediate family, or a close relative.

But this strongly supportive context for healing is not enough. To become a healer, a Kung must first seek *num*. With men, this seeking usually starts at the age of approximately twenty. The young man becomes a student and for several years expresses his search by going to as many dances as possible, perhaps two or three a week. With women, the age of seeking is more variable, the search briefer. But *num* is not "put into" someone who cannot accept it; students must be willing and ready to receive the *num* which can evoke the experience of *kia*. They must learn to "drink *num*" (*chi num*), a phrase used by the Kung to describe the process and act of learning to heal, especially the experience in which *kia* first develops into healing.

170

The teachers are Kung healers. During their non-*kia* state, they remain ordinary persons rather than intimates of the gods or chosen instruments. They do not demand from students either obedience or a long apprenticeship. The period of learning is focused within the dance itself. The emphasis is on experiential education. The core of teaching lies at those points when *kia* is about to occur. The teachers are with the students at the threshold of this experience, trying to help them over their fear and into *kia*, then guiding them to use that *kia* for healing.

Though originally issuing from the gods, *num* now passes regularly from person to person. Teaching is primarily by example. The teachers have been there before. They may or may not experience *kia* at the same time as the students, but certainly they have experienced *kia* many times before.

The principal dance form is the Giraffe, so named because giraffe healing or *num* songs now dominate in it. Gemsbok and Eland songs have also enjoyed a popularity in this dance form, and at times have lent their names to it. But the Giraffe is presently the central form of healing dance among the hunting-gathering Kung.

The more experienced healers do not always need a full Giraffe dance to activate their *num*. Severe and especially chronic illnesses usually precipitate small healings which can hardly be called a dance. One or two healers can *kia* and heal, supported only by their own singing of *num* songs and perhaps by the singing of several women. The actual dancing may be minimal: perhaps a few steps, done mostly in place.

With some chronic conditions, small healings can occur every night of the week and over long periods of time. A wife or husband often treats an ailing spouse in such a manner. Certain experienced healers can also heal themselves while sitting alone at night and singing *num* songs. If the healer's spouse is present, the two may sing to and for each other, healing themselves and each other.

Richard Lee [a collaborator with the author in original field work] has described one such healing. An old woman healed her husband nightly for almost a year. Diagnosed by visiting Western doctors as having cancer, her husband lasted much longer than they had expected. She "fought the battle almost single-handed." Sometimes only her daughter would sing with her. The woman's message to her husband was clear and consistent: "Your dead father is trying to take you away. Those who are still alive have been mean to you. Your dead father is going to deprive them of you. You've been good all your life. I begged your dead father to give those who are still alive another chance to be good to you. Your dead father agreed, and spared you tonight."

Herbal medicines and a healing massage are also used by the Kung, but these are supplementary treatments, usually reserved for less serious or more localized ailments. Neither requires a healing dance or the experience of *kia* for its use.

"Aches and pains" and especially a general "tiredness" can also call for a massage. The healing massage involves forceful manipulation of large areas of the body, concentrating on the shoulders, back, and stomach. The massagers rub their sweat onto the one being healed and periodically shake their hands off into space, expelling the patient's sickness.

Knowledge of herbal medicines and skill with massage are not necessarily possessed by the same person, nor are such capabilities limited to or even possessed by all healers.

The traditional Kung approach to healing is integral to its context in the Kalahari. Woven into the Kung's hunting-gathering lifestyle, the dance seems to highlight it. Time is definitely available for the all-night dances. Community is at the dance, and the dance establishes community. Everyone is welcome at the dance. Parents teach children about *num*. In a real sense, it is the community, in its activation of *num*, which heals and is healed. What Westerners might call the "sacred" and the "profane" merge playfully and dramatically at the dance: the raucous sexual joking as the dancers move toward *kia*; the dialogue between the healer and the spirits, first pleading, then insulting. And there are no restrictions in the access to *num*. In egalitarian fashion, all receive healing. *Num* is shared throughout the community. It is not meant to be hoarded by any one person; perhaps it never can be. There is no limit to *num*. It expands as it boils. As one person reaches *kia* at the dance, others are stimulated to follow. One Kung becoming a healer does not mean another cannot become one; the reverse is true, especially when the two are closely related.

The Kung do not seek *num* for its own sake. They seek its protection and enhancement for the individual, the group, and the culture simultaneously. The healing approach does not undermine the execution of everyday responsibilities. The healer is a hunter or gatherer who also happens to heal. Healing remains harmonious with the different levels of Kung existence. Its effectiveness depends on this context.

The question of whether *kia*-healing "works" depends to a large extent on who asks it. When asked by someone with a contemporary Western scientific orientation, the question usually has a rational, materialistic emphasis. Such a person wants to know what specific illnesses are cured, how rapidly, and how completely. If asked by a Kung, the question would have a more holistic meaning. *Num* is energy, one form of which can be translated as "medicine." For the Kung, healing deals with the whole person, in all aspects and situations. Healing is directed as much toward alleviating physical illness in an individual as toward enhancing the healer's understanding; as much toward resolving conflict in the village as toward establishing a proper relationship with the gods and the cosmos. A healing may be specifically directed toward one of these focuses, but the healing in fact affects them all. For a Kung, the question would be: Does healing "heal," rather than just "cure," and does it heal "sickness" as well as "illness"?

Although the Kung word for "heal" and "cure" is the same (*twe*), as is the word for "illness" and "sickness" (*xai*), the context of usage creates distinctions. "Illness" means a more specific or delimited disease with symptoms, usually manifest. As the Kung see it, all people have sickness in them, which on occasion flares up and is expressed in an illness. This does not mean that every Kung is an ambulatory disease-ridden patient. Rather, each Kung has the potential for illness. When the Kung offer healing to all at the dance, whether they have a manifest illness or not, they are healing sickness, providing in part what Westerners would call "preventative" treatment.

"Healing" is the generic term, including in its meaning, "to cure." The Kung criterion for a cure is that someone with an illness gets better, usually with the relief or disappearance of the symptoms. A supple-

173

mentary criterion is that the healer sees the cause of the illness coming out of the patient. A cure does not occur with every healing effort.

The full range of what in the West would be called physical, psychological, emotional, social, and spiritual illnesses are treated at the healing dance. Nearly every Kung, and many of the neighboring blacks as well, can describe how the healing dance has cured someone. Sometimes the reported cure is dramatic. For example, someone who has been clawed by a leopard and "given up for dead" is healed and recovers miraculously. More often the cure is undramatic. Someone who complains of "chest wheezing and coughing," who is experiencing respiratory congestion from what would in the West be diagnosed as chronic emphysema, is healed and then is able to go about his day in a normal way. A woman who is described as "so weak she is dying," probably with advanced tuberculosis, receives intense healing and has a little more strength the next day. A young woman comes to the dance for healing because her "milk is not coming properly" to her nursing baby. The next day her milk returns. Another woman receives healing at the dance because her lip has become increasingly infected and swollen. After several days, the swelling and infection subside. A healing dance is held for a young healer who complains of "tired blood" and shows signs of great physical and psychological fatigue. At the dance he regains his strength, in part through his own dancing and healing. Or a woman gets relief from the discomforts of her pregnancy. Two families from different camps are in conflict over an upcoming marriage between two of their young people. Accusations of stinginess in regard to some of the gift exchanges required before marriage fill the air. During a healing dance attended by the two families along with the rest of the camps, the tensions subside, though the conflict is not resolved to the total satisfaction of either family.

After spending the night in the intense intimacy of the healing dance, the people will speak of how good it is to be together. The Kung refer to the healing dance as *num chxi*. The sense of *chxi* is "to gather together to sing and dance." "A good dance makes our hearts happy," they say. And a "happy heart"—the expression of spiritual balance—is what heals the people.

174

Navajo Sand Paintings
Re-Creating a Healthy Cosmos

SAM GILL

Navajo sand painting is a ritual procedure in Navajo culture which is part of certain religious ceremonials performed to cure an ailing person. The sand painting is constructed on the floor of a ceremonial hogan and depicts mythic persons who have a connection with the cause of the illness being treated. It must be carefully replicated according to the memory of the officiating singer or medicine man. No visual record is kept by the Navajo people, but hundreds of different patterns are known to exist. The finished picture, like a costume and mask, provides a physical form in which the spiritual beings may manifest their presence. When cornmeal is sprinkled by the singer on the painting and the person for whom the ceremony is being performed, the holy people are present in the sand painting. The rite identifies the ailing person, who walks onto and sits in the middle of the painting, with each of the holy people present in it. The identification is physically accomplished by a transfer of sands on the medicine-moistened hands of the singer, taken from the feet, legs, body, and head of each of the sand-painted figures and pressed on the corresponding body parts of the person sitting on the painting. When this identification is complete, the sand painting, badly defaced during the rite, is completely destroyed by the singer, who scratches through it with a plumed wand. The mixed sands are removed and return to nature.

In the ceremonials in which sand painting rites play a major role, the cause of the illness being treated is attributed to impaired relationships with specific life-giving forces in the Navajo cosmos. These life-giving forces are associated with certain holy people whose powers have become directed against the life forces of the ailing person. In the ceremonial cure, rites are enacted to appease the holy people and persuade them to remove their life-threatening influence. But this in itself does not constitute a cure, for the person must be placed again in a state of order modeled upon the creation of the Navajo world. The sand painting rite is therefore a rite of re-creation in which the person is remade in a way corresponding to the conditions of his or her ailment. In this rite of re-creation, the sand painting is the essential vehicle.

The perspective of the person being re-created is based on his position in the center of the sand painting facing east, the direction of the road of life. This visual perspective on the painting is unique and cannot be shared by anyone. It is a view of the sand painting from within it, being surrounded by it. Only portions of the sand painting may be seen at any one time, and these only from the center outward. To sit upon the sand painting and to be identified with the many holy people and cosmic dimensions which are alive in it is to experience the complexity and diversity, the dynamics and the tensions, represented in the surrounding painting; but it is also to experience the one point common to all, and therefore to see and to feel the diversity and tensions.

The illness suffered is an experience of the world at odds with itself, but this experience is made cosmic when the person finds that this is but an incident in the whole drama of the universe. The illness is overcome when the person realizes (in the largest sense of that term) that in some places these tensions and oppositions can be balanced in a unity that signifies good health and beauty.

But how do we understand the destruction of the painting? We must see that it is not the materials of the sand painting, nor really even the design it takes, that is at the core of its meaning and power. Rather it is the process and use that is made of it that is important. It is a cosmic map. It is a vehicle by which re-creation, health, and beauty in life and the world are achieved. The sufferer finds his or her way to health from within the sand painting, and by becoming a part of it, it disappears and becomes a part of him or her. The picture disappears in the process of a person coming to know the fullness and unity of the reality it represents. The destruction of the picture corresponds to the dissolution of the tensions and imbalances which have given rise to the suffering.

We are now quite used to seeing Navajo sand paintings reproduced in books and articles on varying subjects. But Navajos themselves strictly forbid making representations of sand paintings and they are never kept as aesthetic objects. Even the use of sand painting figures in the sand-glue craft has not met with the approval of most Navajo singers. Sand paintings must be destroyed by sundown on the day they are made. They are not aesthetic objects; they are instruments of a ritual process.

In terms of visual perspective we always view sand paintings from a position which would be directly above and at such a distance that the whole painting is immediately graspable, with each side equidistant from our eyes. This is completely impossible for Navajos. When a painting six feet, or even larger, in diameter is constructed on the floor of a hogan only twenty feet in diameter, the perspective from the periphery is always at an acute angle to the surface. A sand painting cannot be easily seen as a whole. The most important point of view is that of the person being cured, and this person sees the painting from the inside out because he or she sits in the middle of it. These differences are basic and cannot be dismissed. The Navajo view is inseparable from the significance which sand painting has for them.

I think that we can say that for the Navajo the sand painting is not the intended product of the creative process in which it is constructed. The product is a healthy human being or the re-creation of a well-ordered world. The sand painting is but an instrument for this creative act, and perhaps it is the wisdom of the Navajo that it be destroyed in its use so that the obvious aesthetic value of the instrument does not supplant the human and cosmic concern.

The Houngan As Healer

MAYA DEREN

The major role of the houngan, or voudoun priest, in Haiti is medical. It is a role which has been exceedingly misunderstood and much maligned. He has been considered as the primary antagonist to modern medicine. This is not, in fact, so. A person who becomes ill begins, as is normal, by attempting to treat himself. In primitive communities this is often as valid as in the modern culture of patented medicines, for the race could not have survived without a widespread knowledge of herbalism. It is true that that knowledge may have been arrived at by trial and error; and it is true that the form in which the drug is administered—most frequently the brewing of a tea from leaves or roots—is relatively crude. But it is also true that the average Haitian peasant knows which leaves to brew for indigestion, which for a headache, which for a cold. If he wakes up without a voice, he chews on a strong parsley root and this restores it rapidly. If someone is suffering from shock, the Haitians soak coarse salt in a small jigger of rum and let the person drink it. If someone is bleeding badly, they apply a spider's web to the wound and the blood coagulates immediately. If a certain parasite enters under the skin, they know exactly where to insert a pin point and draw it out whole. If a wound is infected, they rub it with garlic, and the sulphur is an effective anti-

179

septic. The peasant midwife is extremely efficient, especially if one considers the very primitive conditions in which she must often function. Basil-leaf water soothes and cools; peppermint leaves are steeped for nausea, etc. They are proud of such knowledge and the remedies are passed down in the family.

If the illness or discomfort does not pass, they consult a houngan. And his first task is to decide whether it is a really physical disease or one of "supernatural" origin. If it is physical, he may attempt to treat it with the more extended knowledge of herbalism to which he has access by summoning his loa, or personal deity, in the govi.* Like the simpler remedies of the peasants themselves, the houngan's treatment is often chemically sound, though crude. But if he sees that the illness is beyond his resources, he will himself recommend that the person get professional medical attention, for it would never be to his credit to fail in a cure. He will even lend the bus fare money for the visit to the dentist or doctor. He himself gets professional medical and dental treatment.

Some of the ailments, such as skin disorders, are the result of malnutrition. If he undertakes merely to relieve these, it is because he knows (as unfortunately many of the health planners do not) that the primary need of the Haitian peasant (particularly in districts such as the vicinity of Port-au-Prince, where the land is drained to feed the city) is more and better food.

It is also true that the Haitian peasant is reluctant to get professional medical attention. But it is not the priest who is the greedy antagonist. The resistance of the Haitian peasant is less against the medicines, which he accepts readily from the houngan or from known friends, than it is against the doctor, as a total stranger. The Haitians prefer their houngan because they trust him. And they trust him not only for religious reasons, but as a human being whom they have known all their lives, whom they have observed under all sorts of conditions, whose personality and character is hence familiar and predictable. They know the percentage of success and failure in his cures. Above all, he lives in their community and is subject to their control: to their approving patronage or the censure of their withdrawal.

*Govi is a red earthen vessel in which the spirits of the dead are lodged. This term is used in reference to sacred vessels as contrasted to canari, which refer to all earthen vessels.

But the professional doctor in the city (and their experiences with the city have not always been pleasant) is a man whom the peasants do not know very well. His dress, his speech, his every gesture emphasizes the distance between their world and his. His professional objectivity contributes to their impression of his human detachment, and they see in this a potential irresponsibility toward them. Small wonder that they are reluctant to surrender themselves to his ministrations.

The free clinic is not as psychologically persuasive as might be imagined. The hard life of the peasant community does not prepare a man for the idea of getting something for nothing. His relationship with his neighbors is based on mutual support and assistance, an exchange of favors. When he pays the houngan, he not only gives money, but also buys a control, a right to demand and expect that he will "get his money's worth." With the free clinic there is no "fair exchange." either social, religious, or financial. He feels he has no control over the doctor, no power to demand results. Conversely, he does not really expect responsibility and efficacy. He does not trust the doctor as a human being, nor does he believe him bound to a fair exchange of responsibility. These attitudes are not metaphysical; they are profoundly logical from the normally human point of view. And no modern doctor would dispute the real importance of a patient's trust.

If the medical profession is to accomplish anything in Haiti, it must begin by abandoning the ancient prejudice against the houngan and relinquishing the melodramatic images of "witch doctors." For one thing, since the recommendations of the houngan are so readily accepted by the people, it might be possible to use him as intermediary for the dispensation of medications. But it is even more important to re-examine his methods and really to understand exactly how he functions within the context with which he is so much more familiar than persons who received their training in the peaceful marble halls of distant universities. It is necessary to remember that his clientele is extremely demanding of actual results and not inclined to grant that professional immunity from the implication of error and failure which is the peculiar code and privilege of doctors in more "sophisticated cultures." And it is especially important to appreciate the real sense of the houngan's distinction between "natural" and "unnatural" disease. One has simply to read "psychosomatic" for the latter term.

No one who has lived long among the peasants could have failed to remark their peculiar conviction of their own frailty. They regard themselves as particularly susceptible to *"grippe"* and *"fievre,"* and they are especially convinced that if a twilight dew which they call *"la sirene"* moistens their head, it will certainly cause at least the *"grippe"* if not some more disastrous ailment. I myself have never been able to remark any perceptible amount of dew at that moment of the day. Yet it is not uncommon for even the strongest men, the same who might beat drums all night, to cover the tops of their heads with a ridiculous little handkerchief against this dampness. One never encounters anything like the contempt for caution which one associates with persons who assume good health as a natural condition. The Haitians seem, on the contrary, to accept the idea that they may easily fall ill, and they are constantly concerned with a variety of precautions. This constant fear is not at all justified by the physical circumstances to which they relate it. And the precautions are such that they could hardly suffice if that threat were really as grave as they say. Actually it is no more than a projection, on to the physical plane, of the profound insecurity and despair with which they live from childhood until death.

For real reasons, which are too numerous to elaborate here, the material situation of most Haitian peasants is, indeed, hopeless. For the time being, at least, the majority of them are doomed to a life without one moment's relief from the most desperate, nerve-racking struggle to eke out daily sustenance. So rarely does an individual achieve some measure of economic gain that the concealment and disguise of such good fortune is the general practice.

Coyote and La Merci, who had for many years been together as common-law man and wife, had long dreamed of being able to afford a regular marriage ceremony, a church ceremony, to be followed by the little "reception," as they called it, for their friends. They had served me loyally and well as domestics, and I had become very fond of them as people. Shortly before I was to leave, I proposed to them that I should pay for such a ceremony, for the new suit and dress, and the reception, as a farewell gift. They were ecstatic. But several days later they approached me shyly, uncertain whether they could make themselves clear. There was nothing they would rather have, they said. But, on the other hand, after my departure, they would return to the country to live in their neighborhood, which, as I knew, was extremely poor. They were afraid, they said, that their neighbors would too much envy their good fortune. And they would overestimate it, thinking that any such advancement actually meant unlimited resources. Things would be stolen from them because people would feel that they had ample funds to replace such articles. They would be plagued for loans of money, and their refusals would be greatly resented. Prices of food would be raised for them specifically, they insisted, because everyone would think they could afford it. They would become altogether suspect. And so, they said, they felt that, in the end, it would give them more trouble than pleasure.

I asked them, then, whether I should use this money to set them up in a little business, to stock a little country store from which they could get started. This, they said, would have similar disadvantages. But cash, I pointed out, would just get used up without anything really to show for it. They nodded and went away. Two days later they appeared with the solution. If I would buy them a cow they said, they could leave it with Coyote's brother, who lived quite far away in another direction. His brother's neighbors would know it did not belong to his brother. And Coyote's neighbors would not know that he had one. And that was, according to them, the real answer.

If the Haitian peasant has some good luck he permits himself only a minimal display, until he is in a position to move up a whole step in the economic scale. Sometimes this concept and practice is even carried to the extent of deliberately scarring a child so that it should not, by its beauty, inspire the evil eye of envy.

The concept of frailty which the Haitian expresses in so many different ways is only his manner of recognizing that his life is spent in a state of precarious balance on the edge of an abyss of despair. (The common "fever" is perhaps ten percent recurrent malaria. For the rest it might be more properly called the fever of despair.) Consequently, even the most minor shock or threat immediately sets in motion a system of defenses which, in a more stable and secure people, would be reserved for only the most critical challenges.

Coyote was a drummer whom I had come to know well from the ceremonies in the Plains district, where he was much in demand. When I returned for a second visit to Haiti, I found a small house in the hills north of Petionville, and proposed to Coyote that he come to "take charge" of my house. I asked him, also, whether he knew of a woman who could do the cooking, and learned, then, for the first time, that he was "married" to La Merci. (The Haitian is so extremely discreet or undemonstrative in public that it would be impossible to guess, at a ceremony, which man was related to which woman.)

As drummer, Coyote had "been around," in the general neighborhood of Port-au-Prince. But for La Merci this employment represented her first real dislocation, as I later found out. In the first days everything seemed to be going very well, and both of them began to make friends in the new neighborhood.

About a week later I noticed that Coyote often brought the coffee, or laid the table (a task usually filled by the woman) and that there seemed to be a good deal of brewing of leaf-teas going on in the little back court. La Merci, it seemed, was not feeling well. She was having pains in her abdomen. But that would shortly be straightened out with these teas. Two day later La Merci was virtually unable to carry out her duties. I suggested consulting a doctor, but this was refused. Instead, an old woman of the neighborhood, who was renowned for her medications, appeared with a bundle of herbs and roots and set about mixing her remedies. These seemed to give La Merci some relief, but it proved to be temporary. That night I heard in their little hut, such moaning and weeping, that I determined to intervene, for the Haitians do not easily express physical hurt. She was in extreme pain and it seemed to me precisely localized at the appendix. On my own initiative I immediately called a physician who arrived and diagnosed it as an acute appendicitis. She was to leave immediately for the hospital, as soon as she had been dressed (for even in her pain she insisted that she wear her very best dress), and the doctor left to prepare for the operation.

In spite of the urgency, La Merci's preparations took a long time, and I could hear a good deal of discussion in the little hut. Finally she emerged, completely dressed, even to her hat, but with the announcement that she would not go to the hospital. "Those who go to the hospital die," she announced. (As a matter of fact, statistically she was correct, since by the time the peasants finally decide to go to the hospital their condition is such that little can be done to save them.) "Besides" she said, "it was a loa who 'cambi—li' [had grabbed her]. It is not for the hospital." Convinced that this was a case where primitive superstition would result in death, I pleaded with her, cajoled, threatened, discharged her, promised rewards, all to no avail. Feeling, finally, that all this excitement would even accelerate the disaster, I permitted her to withdraw to her hut, and I was fully prepared to be summoned to her death-bed during the night.

The next morning she was still alive, and even, it would seem, a little better. I was resigned to my helplessness and let the matter take its course. That evening, while Coyote and I were discussing the situation, the child from next door interrupted to tell us that a loa had mounted the head of his grandmother, and had a special message for Coyote regarding La Merci. We both went next door immediately and saluted the loa. It was an *Ogoun*, the deity of iron or power. La Merci was not, he said, "naturally" sick. The loa had gripped her because she had not properly carried out her last obeisances, upon leaving her ancestral land, where the *cailles Mysteres* of her family stood. Specifically, she had thrown water and "signaled" in only two directions, and the loa were extremely angry over this negligent leave-taking. La Merci, Ogoun said, must return and must ask forgiveness and must propitiate the deities by offering them a chicken. Ogoun then concerned himself with matters pertaining to the other family, and Coyote and I left.

Coyote had been essentially in agreement with me as to the physical nature of the illness. But, as he pointed out, it was impossible to convince La Merci of this, and so it might be well to do as the loa suggested. The loa, he said, would probably accept a cheap chicken this time, if they were promised a better feast upon her final homecoming.

Accordingly, the following morning, La Merci, looking much better already, was given the money for the fare and for the chicken, along with an extra amount, so that she might bring some small gifts to her neighbors. It was a long trip. When she returned the following afternoon she was in high spirits, full of energy, and the stomach-ache was completely gone. She had reaffirmed her ties with her ancestral loa; she did not feel lost any more. And her relationship with everyone was no longer marked by the subtle anxiety which had at first been present.

If a loa had not intervened as diagnostician, a case of such severity would probably have involved the consultation of a houngan, who would have called up his own loa in the govi and discussed the case with him. Having ascertained the reason for her loa's anger, he would also have been instructed about (or would have decided for himself) the curative measures. In cases where the psychosomatic projection may have been carried to the point of organic disturbance, he might have simultaneously given the patient both a herbal treatment, to relieve these effects, and a ritual treatment, to make peace with the loa. It is, in fact, because he often combines the two elements that his treatments have been so misunderstood, for the ritualistic measures are interpreted as directed at the physical ailment, or as an unnecessary embellishment of the herbal cure.

Our general tendency is to regard the psychosomatic act of transferring a difficulty from the psychic to the physical system as "bad." This evaluation reflects, more than would be admitted, a moral dislike of "dishonesty" and a scientific rejection of "untruth." But an organism cares little for such abstract criteria. It is concerned with self-preservation. When a man is threatened by a blow, his instinctive gesture is to raise his arm over his head and face, to protect the most fragile portion of his anatomy, the brain. To receive the blows "honestly" on the head, would soon make him punch-drunk. When a situation is temporarily or permanently and irremediably brutal, the organism behaves like a clever boxer: it shields the mind from the blows which would only destroy it, and absorbs the shock in the muscular and durable flesh. If the Haitian peasant were forced to "face" his hopeless situation, it would be moral suicide for him. What possible moral justification can there be for making a man stare into the jaws of his own death? And where is the medical wisdom of telling a patient that his indigestion, or worse, is due to his own insecurity, or the world situation, and thus brutally destroying the flimsy veil of tolerable discomfort by which the man sought to conceal from himself his intolerable despair?

The methods of the houngan not only respect the essential wisdom of the psychosomatic mechanism, but—and this is the most remarkable feature—use it therapeutically. The diagnosis of "unnatural" or "unphysical" illness is not simply a negative judgment, as it seems to those who conceive only in terms of physical causes. On the contrary, the houngan's main job is to discover the non-physical or unnatural cause. This may be either an act of aggressive evil magic against the person or a punishment for his failure to serve his loa properly. In either case there exists the possibility of a resolution through action of some sort. Instead of the hopeless finality of absolute, abstract despair, the man is immediately involved in the idea of promising action. The very fact that an answering action is inherently indicated is the first therapeutic device which is set into motion. Thus psychosomatic projection serves not as an evasion but as a means of making the moral problem accessible on a level of real action. And it is an accepted fact that activity, hopeful activity, is the only thing which can prevent demoralization and can rehabilitate after shock.

The second therapeutic manipulation consists in the requirement that the action shall not be executed by the priest but *must be carried out, in major portion, by the patient himself*, under guidance of the priest. The patient must himself straighten out his difficulties with the loa. In other words, the patient treats himself, and this is another boost to his morale. Almost inevitably, no matter how ill the person is, he must take part in the rituals relating to his treatment.

Finally, the nature of the action is almost inevitably disciplinarian. It exercises the will, tightens one's forces, focuses the personality into an integration. The salutary effect of the exercise of self-discipline is admittedly remarkable. Instead of accepting an objective destiny with indulgent despair, the Haitian assumes a subjective failure which is accessible to correction. Thus, in the final analysis, the loa and the houngan treat psychic shock through the physical channel and propose the only moral therapy which exists: action and discipline.

The Powwow Doctor

RICHARD E. WENTZ

I remember when they told me. They said that Mammy Wentz pow-wowed for me when I was very little. She had cured me of being "liver-grown." I don't really know what it means to be livergrown; I think it's a form of what used to be called "pleurisy." But I was cured, they said. Mammy was a healer—a powwow doctor, the Pennsylvania Dutch call them. She died when I was about four years old so I don't remember her too well. But after I grew up, left home for college and a place in the world, I often thought of Mammy Wentz (we pro-nounced it "Memmy"). She became a greater and greater mystery as I learned more about the folk culture of my people and about those forms of human behavior we have learned to call "religious."

I have only two images of her. Well, perhaps three; but that's because I have a framed picture of her and Pappy Wentz. Pappy is holding me on his lap, me in my little white dress, aged about three months I suppose. Mammy has on a long dark frock, wears black stockings, sensible tie-up shoes, and horn-rimmed glasses. That image from the picture blends with one I have of her coming over the path through the fields from the woods behind our house. The fields were full of sumac and bitter cherry trees. That's the way Mammy would come to visit me and bring me a nickel.

188

The other image is of Mammy in a casket in the front room of their house. "Front rooms," as they were called, were always off limits except for laying out corpses. Otherwise they were shut up and dark. I never liked front rooms and I suppose I suppressed that image of Mammy in the casket.

It was much, much later that I learned Mammy was a powwow doctor. Susanna Elizabeth was the daughter of Hartman Zeller and Elizabeth Scheirer Zeller, who had come to Pennsylvania from Oedheim, Germany, in 1846. The Zeller family had settled on about forty acres of farm land in Franklin Township, Carbon County. There had been Germans in eastern Pennsylvania for more than a hundred and fifty years before Hartman Zeller came to America. In Penn's Woods they had fashioned a unique culture of their own. They were not merely Germans living in Pennsylvania. They related to their new environment, with its rolling hills and limestone outcroppings, by becoming Pennsylvania Dutch.

The Dutch are really the *deutsch*, or the *deitsch*, as they say it themselves. "Dutch" is not Holland Dutch, but just reflects the inability of the English-speaking inhabitants to pronounce *deutsch* without saying "Dutch." Anyhow, the Pennsylvania Dutch culture is a new blending of German dialect and folk culture, interacting with the English language and the ways of the Scotch-Irish and English people who also lived in eastern Pennsylvania.

The Dutch were basically simple people—farmers, craftsmen, artisans, and maybe a merchant or two. Incidentally, the Dutch were mostly Lutheran and Reformed—"church" Dutch. They didn't (and don't) wear broad-brimmed hats and ride horse and buggy. The latter are the "plain" Dutch, varieties of Mennonite and Amish.

Then there were the Moravians, too, and the Schwenkfelders. But the Dutch were "just folks." They brought with them to Pennsylvania all the old ideas and practices that the people had known for centuries. They knew how to stop a hemorrhage, what herbs to take for dyspepsia. And they knew how to fight off the Evil-Eye and put an enemy in his place with charms and spells. But mostly they knew how to heal, to cure. And they had all kinds of formulas (words and signs appropriately used) and special treatments. People all over the world

189

seem to know these things. Of course, they all have their own words and special ways that somehow relate to the religious tradition of which they're a part.

The Germans who came to Pennsylvania knew, with many of the Jews who had lived among them in Europe, that Moses was much less a prophet than he was a magician. He knew white magic and he was a sorcerer who could make plagues of gnats and flies, boils, hail, locusts, blood and frogs when an enemy tried to oppress him. All the magic that Moses knew had been preserved and passed on. It was useful knowledge that had to be protected. It had to be learned, taught. But only the right people could learn it. It had to be passed on in the right way to the right people. In the villages of Germany there were those who had such special power and magic. Sometimes they kept these things secret—away from the priests and bishops who worried about the orthodoxy of these teachings and practices. But often the authorities accepted the magic. They might practice it themselves. Or they might have need of a healer or a sorcerer sometimes.

The people brought all of this magic to Pennsylvania. And when they got there, they discovered that there were "red men" in the back country who had similar powers. These shamans knew how to enter and interpret the world of dreams where the ways of magic and healing derived their power. They were called "powwows" (*pauwaus*)—"dreamers" in the Algonquian language. Powwowing could heal an ailment or an injury, but it could also heal human relations. What the Native Americans did for healing was not so different from the magic of the Pennsylvania Germans. Maybe some of the Dutch saw themselves as redeeming the power of the Indian powwows. Perhaps they thought of themselves as true powwows. Whatever the reason, and the history is not very clear, the Pennsylvania Dutch healers became "powwows." Mammy Wentz was a powwow doctor.

The most familiar handbook for powwowing is Johann Georg Hohmann's *Lang Verborgener Freund, The Long Hidden Friend,* with a strung-out subtitle: *Wonderful and Well-Tried Remedies and Magic Arts, as Well for Man as Beast, with Many Proofs Shown in This Book, of Which Most Are As Yet Little Known, and Appearing Now for the First Time in America.* The book was probably first published in Reading around 1820, then Harrisburg and Carlisle, through its many editions. Along with some secret texts attributed to Moses, this collection of folk remedies is basic to the art of powwow, and tradition traces it back to Albertus Magnus in the thirteenth century.

In his Preface, Hohmann justifies publication of the book in the face of opposition from unbelievers and clergy alike: "Many people in America believe in no hell or heaven. In Germany such people are fewer. I, Hohmann, ask who cures wounds and gangrene? Who stops blood? I answer; and I, Hohmann, say: The Lord does it. Therefore there is a hell and a heaven. I don't think much of such people." Hohmann's logic may leave us reeling, but he speaks the logic of the folk, who know that everything exists for a reason, that life is an affair of adjustment, give and take, no matter what the educated people may say. The Pennsylvania Dutch believe that too much "fancy learning" gets a person all "ferhoodled" or "oofgabollixed"—all mixed up.

Some powwows were specialists who were widely known for their success with certain ailments. Sometimes the powwow gave the patient a small muslin bag. Inside was a piece of paper with curing words written in German. Perhaps the writing was inverted, so that it could be read only in a mirror. An amulet like this prepared on St. John's Eve or Christmas Eve was especially powerful. You would wear it around your neck on a string, or pinned to your underwear. On the bag in red ink were the letters INRI, symbolic abbreviation for Jesus of Nazareth, King of the Jews. A row of four Latin crosses nested below INRI, and underneath that the Christian name of the patient, below that the surname.

Hohmann's *Long Hidden Friend* is a compilation of traditional healing charms and formulae that are ancient in origin. The people have had their own way of passing on the wisdom and the magical power itself. Mammy Wentz was taught the art of powwow by a male of the previous generation, an art she could transmit only to a male of the next generation. Sometimes I wish I had been Mammy's initiate, because I have discovered that healing is a cosmic affair, that life is worth living when you know how to use words and actions that have no utilitarian or functional value whatever. The charms and the actions of the folk are not very sophisticated—they belong to the people. They help the people to have a hand in restoring the proper order.

There are very few powwow doctors in Pennsylvania anymore. Most of the people are satisfied with the automobile as the model for health and healing. You buy one, you feed it, you pay for it. When something goes wrong, you open it up, take the bad piece out and put a new one in. You go on your way, hoping that an insurance company will pay most of the exorbitant cost. Your health, like the health of the car, is a private matter between you and the mechanic. It has little to do with people, with ancient wisdom, with relationship to the whole order of things. We no longer understand that healing is salving—salvation.

If Mammy had not healed me when I was a baby, I would probably not know how to smile and laugh at this silly world with all its pretense. I would probably not know how to accept a childhood that was anything but pleasant most of the time. I would probably not know how to love Mammy and Pappy, and a tormented father whose own life was filled with fear and misery. I would still think these people were ignorant and superstitious.

Sometimes, when you visit a village in the Pennsylvania Dutch country, you will still see a mother pick up a crying child who has skinned his knee on the sidewalk: "Come, come, Booblie, Mamma will powwow for it and make it all well." Then she will make some signs over the knee and mumble some strange words. Little "Chonnie" will stop crying and run back to play. And when I get angry at someone who has become my enemy, I sometimes wish I knew how to use the powwow charm against evil spirits.

PART V

Letting Go

Mahasamadhi of Ramana Maharshi

Arthur Osborne

For several years before the body's end, at least from 1947 onwards, the health of Sri Bhagavan had caused alarm. Rheumatism had not only crippled his legs but attacked his back and shoulders also. Even apart from that, there was an impression of great weakness, although he himself refused to take notice of it. It was felt that he needed a more nutritious diet than the ashram food, but he would not consent to take anything extra.

He was not yet seventy but looked much more aged. Not careworn, for there was absolutely no sign of care—he had known none. Just aged and very frail. Why was it that one who had been vigorous and robust, who had known little sickness in life and no grief or care, should have aged so much beyond his years? He that taketh upon himself the sins of the world—he who alleviates the karma of the devotees—it was only by himself drinking the poison churned up that Siva could save the world from destruction. Sri Shankara wrote: "Oh Sambhu, Lord of life! Thou bearest also the burden of Thy devotees' temporal life."

There were many signs, always inconspicuous, how, even physically, Sri Bhagavan bore the burden. A devotee, Krishnamurthi by name, has related in a Tamil journal issued by Janaki Ammal, a lady devotee, how he went and sat in the hall one day when he had a severe pain in the index finger. He told no one, but to his surprise, he saw Sri Bhagavan hold and rub the same finger on his own hand, and the pain disappeared. Many others have known similar relief.

For Sri Bhagavan life on Earth was no treasure to be economized; it was indifferent to him how long it lasted. There was once a discussion in the hall as to how long he would live. Some quoted the astrologers as saying that he would live to be eighty; others either denied the accuracy of astrology or doubted its applicability to Sri Bhagavan who had no more karma to work out. He listened to the discussion, smiling but taking no part in it. A newcomer, puzzled by this, asked, "What does Bhagavan think about it?" He did not reply but smiled approvingly when Devaraja Mudaliar replied for him, "Bhagavan does not think about it." The whole last year of his life was an illustration of this. The devotees grieved over the suffering and dreaded the threatened death; he did not.

Early in 1949 a small nodule appeared below the elbow of his left arm. It was not considered serious, but in February the ashram doctor cut it out. Within a month it returned, larger and more painful, and this time it was recognized as a malignant tumor and caused general alarm. Towards the end of March doctors came from Madras and operated. The wound did not heal up properly and the tumor soon began to grow again, larger and higher up.

Henceforth there was an air of tragedy and inevitability about the march of events. The orthodox medical men let it be known that they could not cure the tumor but could only operate and that it might return again, despite radium treatment and, if it did, would eventually prove fatal. Those of other schools believed that they could cure it and that operating would only bring it back in a worse form, as in fact happened, but they were not allowed to try in time.

When the tumor returned after the March operation the doctors suggested amputating the arm, but there is a tradition that the body of a Gnani should not be mutilated. Indeed, it should not be pierced with metal and even the operation had been a breach of tradition. Sri Bhagavan had submitted to that but he refused the amputation. "There is no cause for alarm. The body itself is a disease; let it have its natural end. Why mutilate it? Simple dressing of the part is enough."

His saying "there is no cause for alarm" led to the hope that he would recover, despite the words that followed and despite the medical opinion; but for him death was no cause for alarm

He also gave rise to hope by saying, "Everything will come right in due course." But in fact it was for us to perceive the rightness of what occurred; he never doubted it.

About this time he translated into Tamil verse a stanza from the *Bhagavatam* (Skandha XI, ch. 13, sloka 36), "Let the body, the result of fructifying karma, remain still or move about, live or die, the Sage who has realized the Self is not aware or it, just as one in a drunken stupor is not aware of his clothing."

Some time later he expounded a verse from the Yoga Vasishtam: "The *Gnani* who has found himself as formless pure Awareness is unaffected though the body be cleft with a sword. Sugar candy does not lose its sweetness though broken or crushed."

Did Sri Bhagavan really suffer? He said to one devotee: "They take this body for Bhagavan and attribute suffering to him. What a pity!" And to one of the attendants he said, "Where is pain if there is no mind?" And yet he showed normal physical reactions and normal sensitivity to heat and cold, and a devotee, S.S. Cohen, records him as having said years earlier, "If the hand of the *Gnani* were cut with a knife there would be pain as with anyone else but because his mind is in bliss he does not feel the pain as acutely as others do." It is not that the body of the *Gnani* does not suffer injury but that he does not identify himself with the body. The doctors and some of the attendants were convinced that there was pain and that, in the later stages, it was excruciating. Indeed, the doctors were amazed at Sri Bhagavan's indifference to pain, at his complete unconcern, even during an operation.

The question of his suffering, like the question of our karma, exists only from the point of view of duality; from his point of view, the point of view of Advaita, neither had any reality. It was with this meaning that he said more than once to devotees, "I am only ill if you think I am; if you think I am well I shall be well." So long as a devotee believed in the reality of his own body and its suffering, so long, for him, the body of the Master was real and suffered also.

For a week or two after the March operation a village herbalist was allowed to try his treatment, but it brought no cure. Sri Bhagavan said to another aspirant who was passed over, "I hope you don't mind when you have taken so much trouble with your medicines." It was never any thought of his own condition, only consideration for those who wished to treat him and loyalty to whatever doctor was in charge. Occasionally he protested at the amount of attention bestowed on his body Several times when there seemed to be an improvement he declared that he wanted no more treatment.

The tumor, diagnosed now as a sarcoma, sapped his little remaining vitality; and yet even as he weakened his face grew gentler, more gracious, more radiantly beautiful. At times his beauty was almost painful to behold.

The arm was heavy and inflamed and the tumor growing. Occasionally he would admit "There is pain" but he would never say "I have pain." In August a third operation was carried out and the wound treated with radium in the hope of destroying the affected tissues and preventing the return of the tumor. The same afternoon, a few hours after the operation, Sri Bhagavan was so gracious as to sit on the veranda of the dispensary where it had been performed, so that the devotees could file past and have *darshan*. One could see that he was exhausted but there was no sign of suffering in his face. I had come for the day from Madras, and as I stood before him the radiance of his smile was such that even exhaustion ceased to be visible. At noon next day he returned to the hall so as not to inconvenience other patients by occupying the dispensary.

There was also a deeper sense of inevitability, far beyond the medical: that Sri Bhagavan knew what was appropriate and sought to give us strength to endure his body's death. Indeed, this long, painful sickness came to appear as a means of preparing us for the inevitable parting which many had first felt they would not be able to endure. Kitty, who was at a boarding school in the hills, was told about it in a letter and wrote back, "I am so very sorry to hear about it. But Bhagavan knows what is best for us." Her letter was shown to him and his face was radiant with pleasure as he commended her wisdom for saying, "What is best for us," not "What is best for him."

He had immense compassion for those who grieved over the suffering and he sought to appease their grief, not the easy way by
removing the suffering and postponing death for a few more years, but
the fundamental way by making them realize that the body was not
Bhagavan. "They take this body for Bhagavan and attribute suffering
to him. What a pity! They are despondent that Bhagavan is going to
leave them and go away—where can he go, and how?"

For some weeks after the August operation there seemed to be an
improvement, but in November the tumor appeared again; higher up
the arm, near the shoulder. In December the fourth and last operation
was carried out. The wound from this never healed. The doctors
admitted now that they could do no more. The case was hopeless, and
if the tumor returned again they could only administer palliatives.

Jayanti fell on January 5th, 1950. Sorrowful crowds gathered for
this his seventieth birthday, which most now felt to be his last. He
gave *darshan* and listened to many new songs composed in his praise.
Some he read through. The temple elephant from town came and
bowed down before him and touched his feet with its trunk. A Rani
from North India was allowed to take a motion picture of the scene.
There was festivity but with an underlying sadness of apprehension.

Many felt already that it was a matter of weeks or days. Now that
the case had been pronounced hopeless Sri Bhagavan was asked to
say himself what treatment should be tried. He said: "Have I ever
asked for any treatment? It is you who want this and that for me, so it
is for you to agree about it among yourselves. If I were asked I should
always say, as I have said from the beginning, that no treatment is
necessary. Let things take their course."

Only after this homeopathy was tried and then Ayurveda, but it
was too late.

Sri Bhagavan kept to his normal daily routine until it became
physically impossible. He took his morning bath an hour before sunrise, sat up to give *darshan*. A small bathroom with an anteroom had
been constructed across the drive just east of the hall, and towards the
end he remained there. There was a narrow little veranda outside
where his couch was put and right up to the end the devotees whom
his sickness had drawn in their hundreds to Tiruvannamalai still had

darshan. He would let nothing interrupt this so long as it was still possible. The devotees would sit morning and afternoon on the hall veranda facing him. Later, when he had grown too weak for that, they would file past the open door of his room, morning and evening. One day his condition caused alarm and the *darshan* was stopped, but as soon as he was able to take notice he expressed displeasure and ordered it to be resumed.

A group of devotees daily chanted prayers and devotional songs for his recovery. He was asked about their efficacy, and replied, smiling, "It is certainly desirable to be engaged in good activities; let them continue."

The tumor returned just above the unhealed wound. It was up near the shoulder now and the whole system was poisoned, so that severe anemia set in. The doctors said the pain must be terrible. He could take scarcely any nourishment. Occasionally he was heard to moan in his sleep but he gave no other sign of pain. From time to time the doctors came from Madras to see him and he was courteous and hospitable as ever. Right up to the end his first question was whether they had received food, whether they were well looked after.

His sense of humor also remained. He would joke about the tumor as though it was something that did not concern him. A woman, in her grief, beat her head against a pillar near the room and he looked surprised and then said, "Oh, I thought she was trying to break a coconut."

Speaking to the attendants and to Dr. T.N. Krishnaswami, doctor and devotee, he explained: "The body is like a banana-leaf on which all kinds of delicious food have been served. After we have eaten the food from it, do we take the leaf and preserve it? Do we not throw it away now that it has served its purpose?"

On another occasion he said to the attendants: "Who is to carry this load of a body even after it needs assistance in everything? Do you expect me to carry this load that it would take four men to carry?"

And to some of the devotees: "Suppose you go to a firewood depot and buy a bundle of firewood and engage a coolie to carry it to your house. As you walk along with him he will be anxiously looking forward to his destination so that he can throw off his burden and get relief. In the same way the *Gnani* is anxious to throw off his mortal body." And then he corrected the explanation: "This exposition is all right as far as it goes, but strictly speaking even this is not quite accurate. The *Gnani* is not even anxious to shed his body; he is indifferent alike to the existence or non-existence of the body, being almost unaware or it."

Once, unasked, he defined *Moksha* (Liberation) to one of the attendants. "Do you know what *Moksha* is? Getting rid of non-existent misery and attaining the Bliss which is always there, that is *Moksha.*"

It was hard to give up hope that even if the doctors failed he might still put aside the sickness by his own power. A devotee begged him to give but a single thought to the desirability of getting well, as this would have been enough, but he replied, almost scornfully, "Who could have such a thought!"

And to others who asked him simply to will his recovery he said, "Who is there to will this?" The "other," the individual that could oppose the course of destiny, no longer existed in him; it was the "nonexistent misery" that he had got rid of.

Some of the devotees made it a plea for their own welfare. "What is to become of us without Bhagavan? We are too weak to look after ourselves; we depend on his Grace for everything." And he replied, "You attach too much importance to the body," clearly implying that the end of his body would not interrupt the Grace and guidance.

In the same vein he said: "They say that I am dying but I am not going away. Where could I go? I am here."

Mrs. Taleyarkhan, a Parsi devotee, besought him: "Bhagavan! Give this sickness to me instead. Let me bear it!" And he replied, "And who gave it to me?"

Then who gave it to him? Was it not the poison of our karma?

A Swedish sadhu had a dream in which the afflicted arm opened and he saw there the head of a woman with grey hair dishevelled. This was interpreted to mean that it was the karma of his mother that he assumed when he gave her *Moksha*, but others saw the woman to signify all mankind or Maya itself.

On Thursday, April 13th, a doctor brought Sri Bhagavan a palliative to relieve the congestion in the lungs but he refused it. "It is not necessary; everything will come right within two days."

That night he bade his attendants go and sleep or meditate and leave him alone.

On Friday the doctors and attendants knew it was the last day. In the morning he again bade them go and meditate. About noon, when liquid food was brought for him, he asked the time, punctual as ever, but then added, "But henceforth time doesn't matter."

Delicately expressing recognition of their long years of service, he said to the attendants, "The English have a word 'thanks' but we only say *santosham* (I am pleased)."

In the morning the long crowd filed past the open doorway, silent with grief and apprehension, and again between four and five in the evening. The disease-racked body they saw there was shrunken, the ribs protruding, the skin blackened; it was a pitiable vestige of pain. And yet at some time during these last few days each devotee received a direct, luminous, penetrating look of recognition which he felt as a parting infusion of Grace.

After *darshan* that evening the devotees did not disperse to their homes. Apprehension held them there. At about sunset Sri Bhagavan told the attendants to sit him up. They knew already that every movement, every touch was painful, but he told them not to worry about that. He sat with one of the attendants supporting his head. A doctor began to give him oxygen but with a wave of his right hand he motioned him away. There were about a dozen persons in the small room, doctors and attendants.

Two of the attendants were fanning him, and the devotees outside gazed spell-bound at the moving fans through the window, a sign that there was still a living body to fan. A reporter of a large American magazine moved about restlessly, uneasy at having been impressed despite himself and determined not to write his story till he got away from Tiruvannamalai to conditions that he considered normal. With him was a French press-photographer.

Unexpectedly, a group of devotees sitting on the veranda outside the hall began singing "*Arunachala-Siva.*" On hearing it, Sri Bhagavan's eyes opened and shone. He gave a brief smile of indescribable tenderness. From the outer edges of his eyes tears of bliss rolled down. One more deep breath, and no more. There was no struggle, no spasm, no other sign of death: only that the next breath did not come.

For a few moments people stood bewildered. The singing continued. The French press-photographer came up to me and asked at what precise minute it had happened. Resenting it as journalistic callousness, I replied brusquely that I did not know, and then I suddenly recalled Sri Bhagavan's unfailing courtesy and answered precisely that it was 8:47. He said, and I could hear now that he was excited, that he had been pacing the road outside and at that very moment an enormous star had trailed slowly across the sky. Many had seen it, even as far away as Madras, and felt what it portended. It passed to the northeast towards the peak of Arunachala.

Letting Go

An Interview with Helen M. Luke

LORRAINE KISLY: You expressed some uneasiness when I told you the theme of this issue of PARABOLA was to be "Wholeness," and suggested that it might be better if it were called "Approaching Wholeness." Why is that?

HELEN LUKE: I think my feeling is that very few people in any generation do actually come to what we could call wholeness incarnate. There may be a lot more who do so just before they die. But as long as we are in linear time, it cannot be put into words, or talked about really by anyone who is still on the way. There are moments for all of us, I think, when we break out beyond that and have a glimpse of what it is, but the few great ones—those whom the East would call Buddhas, whom we would call those who live the Christ within all the time—are very, very rare. But they do exist. And I do think we should talk about our intuitions of wholeness. This is very important in the beginning. Once one knows it is there, one can be absolutely certain of meaning in life—and go along whatever one's way is, trying to remember. We're so apt to forget.

L.K.: It's curious what it is in us which does remember.

H.L.: There is something which remembers—it's always there. I don't think anyone who has once experienced it would ever forget entirely. Although it can turn negative.

L.K.: In what way?

H.L: When it's swallowed up by a power drive from the ego.

L.K.: The glimpse itself can become an obstacle?

H.L.: Well, wholeness must include everything. It is our choice as human beings as to whether we experience it positively or negatively. You may have read Charles Williams' *Descent Into Hell*. It's so clear there that Wentworth, who ends up in a state of hell, does so by small choices along the way. He is absorbed *into* wholeness, though he as a unique person no longer exists. After all, Dante made it very clear that hell is a choice. People who were in his Hell, if offered Heaven, would not and could not choose it.

L.K.: You have written that people do get what it is that they want. Why do you think it is that so few seem to choose the path toward wholeness—that so many choose peace, perhaps, rather than struggle?

H.L.: It could be said, I think, that we all try to choose peace, but that many move further and further away from it by evasion of the struggles and necessary conflicts of the human journey. What the one on the way to hell chooses all the time is peace for himself, rejection of everybody else except his own ego; like Wentworth, he chooses his own images of a lover instead of an actual lover, and so on. The point about peace is that the true peace does not come until one has been through *all* the struggles of the ego, and until one has accepted boundaries and conflict—to the bitter end. That's what the whole Christian story is about. That's what the cross is.

L.K.: Jung has written that what we call consciousness is just a tiny island in the vast and deep sea of the psyche, and that man is a small part of the whole and can never really know it. So we are limited in many ways.

H.L.: Yes, because we are still centered in the ego, you see: I find it very interesting that you are doing this [tenth anniversary] issue on "Wholeness" after your first issue, which was on "The Hero." We all have to experience at first the strengthening of the ego, the development of its ability to discriminate, to make choices, to get into trouble, to get out of it, and so on. And then comes a point when one has to sacrifice the hero. The hero himself has had to make his sacrifices along the way in order to defeat the dragon, to achieve his aim. Now this in Jungian terms would be the journey of the ego getting to know its shadow side—all the parts that have been repressed, both good and bad. It isn't that the shadow is only the dark elements which we think are wicked, because one can also repress one's positive abilities if one does not want to take the responsibility of living them. But there comes a time when the ego relatively knows all it can, has come to terms with its dark sides, can recognize when it is being possessed by projections, and so on. And when that work is largely done—and this I think is a very important moment on Jung's way of individuation, as he called it—there comes a time when we must sacrifice the will to achieve, the time when we then have to let go. It's what Lao Tzu says—that when you are pursuing learning you gain something every day, but when you turn to the Tao—which means wholeness, really—then you drop something every day, you let go of something every day. It's a letting go process, and it takes usually many years, letting go by degrees. For instance, if you don't begin to let go of your will to be successful, to achieve in the outer world—or anywhere else, for that matter, the inner world too—you will go on saying that you must get better and better every day, the ego will go on saying it. What begins that process of letting go is when you can really experience the difference between the ego—that little light of consciousness that we have—and the Self, which is the whole Self, the whole sphere and also the center. The Self is a Jungian term, in India it is the Atman, and in the West the Christ within, the divine wholeness both immanent in every unique human being and at the same time transcendent and universal. If you are still identified with the ego, after you have had a glimpse of the Self, then you may begin to be possessed by a drive for power even if you weren't before. This is how so many cults develop. The leader had a very real vision at one time as a young man, but then he begins to teach it and it becomes identified with his personal ego. Now in each one of us this can easily happen, to some degree.

L.K.: In the hero's journey, then, it is necessary to develop the ego very strongly so that there is then something which can let go?

H.L.: Exactly; through the ego's choices the inner vision becomes incarnate. In a recent book by Russell Lockhart, *Words As Eggs*, he asks in the introduction, what are we to do after we have done the absolutely necessary work of coming to terms with the shadow, with the "animus" and "anima," the masculine in a woman, the feminine in a man, the inner figures? We can now recognize them and know when one of them starts playing tricks and so on—what do we do then? It seems that very often psychologists are not clear when the religious side must take over; not in the literal church sense, but in the deepest spiritual sense.

L.K.: In all your work I feel a kind of interdependence between the way of Jung, turning to what is dark, what is hidden, and the Christian way of turning toward the light of Logos. I don't know if you feel this is so.

H.L.: Yes, but when you say the light of Logos, do you mean God? Well, don't call it Logos, because the Self is not just Logos, it is Eros as well, and indeed, the Self is the unity of opposites. It is the truth of Christianity, too, but you rightly say that Christians so often mistake the light of Logos for the whole. Jung pointed out the absolute necessity for the feminine values without which there would be no perception of Self. This is especially true in our time when everything is geared toward achievement. One of the best antidotes to that is to read Lao Tzu, I think: "When you do nothing, everything is done." And it's true—if you are talking on the right level. But it's mostly not understood. You see, it is so much a matter of levels. Of course cause and effect and all that comes from them operate in our daily lives on that level the whole time. But it cannot really have a meaning—and that's our great danger—unless we recognize that time itself doesn't exist. That's what physicists are now telling us. It is a very exciting thing in our time, modern physics, which is confirming everything that the East has known for thousands of years.

L.K.: The fact that something can be true on one level, and utterly false on another, causes a great deal of confusion, I think. And also the inaccessibility of a level higher than one is on.

H.L.: Yes. The point of the second half of life, then, is to discover that level which makes all the other levels distinct, yet one in the whole. I have seen as I get *really* old that something fascinating begins to happen. It happens, as everybody knows, that you begin to remember early things in your life very vividly—and then you are apt to forget things that happened yesterday because they're not important anymore somehow. My view is that you do remember things that are really vital, but you forget much that isn't. At any rate, you remember the early things. And then there is, so to speak, a choice: you can either let that state, as so many people naturally do, become nostalgia, or even senility, or what can happen is that those memories suddenly acquire an enormously enhanced meaning in the whole of your life. You begin to see your life as a circle instead of as a straight line. That's just one place where you begin to find that level where everything is a circle. But we have to walk on the straight lines, and we have to experience fully the horizontal and the vertical, the earth and the spirit, and the meeting point at the center before that can happen.

L.K.: In Carlos Castaneda's book, Don Juan called old age the last enemy, and your description of how that last enemy is overcome is quite different from images of fighting against it, denying it—or simply sinking into it. You are saying that it is a time for continuing to grow—a very important kind of new growth.

H.L.: That's the vital thing, and you can only do that by letting things go, not by holding on. It comes, in my experience, little by little, in allowing outer responsibilities to drop away at the right times. But more and more—and I think this is most important—it becomes a matter of turning our attention to the smallest things. I can so easily feel that I have to get over with washing the dishes or whatever needs doing around the house in order to get down to doing what is really important—to sit down and write, or meditate, or whatever! After you let go the hero who wants to kill the dragon and go out and conquer, the task becomes a matter of full attention to the smallest fact. And you can catch yourself rejecting a fact. Over and over. Whether it is the fact of this table, or the fact of having slipped and fallen, or whatever may happen to you, or the world, or anything else, but also the fact of the chair you are sitting in. The whole either doesn't exist, or it exists in everything. We are forever trying to exclude the ego's failures—to exclude in order to find our peace that way. But to find our peace by including everything dark and light, is a very great suffering for the ego, because it has to give up all its will to dominate. The ego doesn't get any weaker; in fact, it probably gets a lot stronger, and the darkness becomes much darker as consciousness becomes greater. But both are facts. And without both, one cannot come near to that level where wholeness can be lived—at least some of the time!

L.K.: Gurdjieff said, "The bigger the angel, the bigger the devil."

H.L.: Exactly so. Wasn't it Rilke who refused to go see Freud or to go into analysis because he said that they might take away his devils, but they'd also take away his angels? And that's true, with most analysis. It can happen when analysis is geared to making someone feel good in the world, adjusted and all the rest. That's the great difference in Jung—he's not concerned about whether you are terribly well adjusted in the world, because what he's interested in is the psyche in its relationship to the Self. The ego is terribly important—it's still complex, it's still there—but it can become one with the Self without losing its uniqueness. That's the marvelous thing.

L.K.: I have a question here about how words can mean such different things, for example "relationship" and "dependence," which on the one hand can mean an excuse and an escape—to lose oneself in relationship with another, to escape responsibility in dependence. On the other hand there is true relationship and real dependence, arising from the facts you were just speaking of. Related to this is the child who appears to have a kind of wholeness and integrity, and the adult, who seems to have to go through a process of fragmentation and division before the meaning of relationship and dependence can become so utterly different.

H.L.: Yes, that really is the point. The enormous difference is that when you begin to know yourself and to glimpse the Self—the wholeness in which all relationship is free and yet essential—you are no longer relating through projection. The child is simply unconsciously one with the wholeness of everything. As soon as it begins to say "I," then comes the beginning of that kind of dependence which is projection. There is a kind of magical attraction from the unconscious. You are part of an archetypal situation—mother and child, and so on. The work of gaining consciousness is to free yourself from identification with one person or another. If you find you hate a person or that there is something that makes you absolutely furious, you may be perfectly sure that it is a part of yourself that is projected there—no matter how true it may be that the other person is behaving badly. You could see that without getting all het up about it. It's normal that one should be angry at things that go on, but there's quite a different quality in that anger if you have ceased to project. If you are projecting you are incapable of compassion, you are incapable of understanding that this person is behaving in this way for reasons that you cannot see, from problems that you know nothing about, but that we all share.

L.K.: Just to be sure I'm clear here, projection is really a kind of identification of yourself with the other?

H.L.: And you don't do it deliberately. It just happens. Projection is the way you see everything that is unconscious in yourself. If you didn't have that projection, you'd never see it. You wouldn't even know you had it. Once you begin to take projections back, this magical kind of tie changes. Once you begin to let go—and this takes a great deal of hard work and watching, and attention and humility: when once you can ask what is it in me that *must* have this to depend on—the minute you begin to make that separation between yourself and that projection, it may then become a sense of relationship. This is so even if it is a relationship with something you dislike and will go

210

on disliking—no one is trying to tell you that you ought to feel differently in that sense—but it will also be compassionate. That, I believe, is what the East means by saying all is emptiness, all is compassion. Not just emptiness—nothing there—but filled with compassion, which is a suffering with whatever is involved. You see the difference? It doesn't mean you can do without relationship: very much the opposite. But you recognize that relationship cannot happen until you are separate. Otherwise it is jut a mixup in the unconscious of two people. You have to separate in order to unite, because uniting means two unique things that meet. Not two fuzzy things—that merge!

That gradual letting go still has to have a context. I think it's enormously important to realize as we work with dreams and the unconscious and other people do the same kind of work in different ways, that when you have an insight it's not enough just to understand. It has then somehow to be put into actual life. It has to be incarnate. This is the true meaning of Christianity. Someone will say he or she has had a big dream and that she feels what it means and so on—she or he must do *something* with it, write it down, paint it, do something *in this world* with it, and after that let it take effect in daily life. It has to make a change, however tiny. This is nearly always a letting go of something. It's all a preparation, of course, for the final letting go of death.

L.K.: You have written something about forgiveness that I wanted to ask you about. You wrote, "...it is the breakthrough of forgiveness, in its most profound sense—universal and particular, impersonal and personal—that alone brings the 'letting go,' the ultimate freedom of the spirit. For in the moment of that realization every false guilt, whether seen as one's own or as other people's, is gone forever—and the real guilt which each of us carries, of refusal to see, to be aware, is accepted. So we may look open-eyed at ourselves and the world and suffer the pain and joy of the divine conflict which is the human condition, the meaning of incarnation." It seems that something must appear to make this possible, to make one *able*.

H.L.: It may appear in something that happens to you, comes to you from the outer world, or it may appear from something that comes to you suddenly from the inner world. It will happen through a long history of choices in small things. The unwillingness to see is to say "no" to life, to the risk of mistakes, to facts.

L.K.: Do you think that with all the difficulties something helps as well?

H.L.: Oh, of course! The difficulties are what help most!

L.K.: I mean that the right difficulties are brought to you at the right time.

H.L.: I think that if one has faith in the meaning of life at all, that is a certainty.

L.K.: It's all arranged?

H.L.: I don't like the word "arranged." It just *is*. It's your fate, and you have a choice how to live it. The East would call it your karma.

L.K.: I have a question about what is really one's own. Certainly all the energies of youth are given, one's talents, weaknesses, and so on are given, but they all seem like raw material. Is there something at the end which could be there and have the taste of being one's own?

H.L.: Your own—how do you mean that? That seems to be a matter of discrimination in the use of words. How does St. Paul put it? "Having nothing, yet possessing all things." Now I would rather have it the other way round, as possessing nothing, yet having all things, because there are so many negative meanings to possession. But it means the same thing, of course. In the ultimate wholeness we surely have everything, but we don't have it exclusively. It isn't ours and not somebody else's. That's the difference, and that is the letting go. You don't any longer feel, "I have the right to do this." You don't have rights, you don't have demands, you don't have wishes. No, that's not true, your ego has them all the time! Don't think you are going to lose your ego's carryings-on; you're not. You merely are not moved by them in the old way. Less and less are they the center of your life. They operate on a certain level, but they become less and less demanding—of people, of things, of everything. Meister Eckhart said we must let go even to the demand to know God. Then it becomes yours. Then it is given to you—when it is completely let go.

L.K.: Well, there seems to be some sort of task that we have in the course of our lives, and there must be an enormous difference between a person who achieves this aim and one who does not. As we are, this remains only a possibility in us.

H.L.: It's a possibility, and it is enormously important for the whole world that some individuals grow to a deep and full consciousness.

L.K.: Is there something which characterizes the way towards this?

H.L.: I think there is something that one can notice in one's own life very clearly. There comes a point when an utterly different kind of suffering is possible, not a neurotic suffering. At the same time that one begins to move beyond the hero/villain stage, one no longer goes up and down into exaltations and depressions. It is the kind of suffering that comes when you accept the fact of whatever it is—a depression is when you don't accept the fact. The suffering which is not a depression can bring a deeper darkness, but it doesn't affect your behavior or those around you. The weight is gone, because there will also be a kind of joy that goes with it, which is nothing emotional. There is a possibility to move beyond being dominated by your emotions. That's the mistake people always make—we think we always have to be improving the ego. We don't. We have to put it through its journey of knowing itself and understanding itself, and so on, and then we shall recognize that its emotions are not objective. They are purely subjective, which is a necessary stage. But then comes what Jung calls objective cognition, and the kind of love he writes about in his autobiography, *Memories, Dreams, Reflections*. The love that is beyond all desiring, all emotions; and that is whole in itself because nothing is excluded.

L.K.: Feeling without emotion?

H.L.: None of these words somehow express it because it is a stage of being, a state of the soul. In fact, it is reality itself. But one just glimpses these things, now and then.

213

L.K.: It is a long way from how compassion is sometimes understood—as a sea of emotionality.

H.L.: The feeling of wishing to save the world comes very often out of a wish to escape from having compassion on your own darkness, for what is inside yourself. If you don't start there you will never have true compassion. First comes compassion for your own weaknesses, and then for the person next to you. Now that doesn't mean that we shouldn't support causes—what matters is *who* supports the causes. You may have to fight, but if you don't fight with forgiveness and compassion, you simply are recreating the same situation. One opposite always creates the other, unless you begin to let go of both of them, then both can become real in a unity which is beyond them.

L.K.: What you say brings to mind the words of Dame Julian of Norwich which you've written about. "All shall be well by the purification of the motive in the ground of our beseeching."

H.L.: That's really the point, isn't it, "By the purification of the motive..." Actually this quotation is from T.S. Eliot's "Four Quartets." The motive—that which moves us from the very ground of our being—is slowly purified here in time through the individual's commitment to the emptying process which is the quest of wholeness. Then, in Lady Julian's words, "All shall be well, and all manner of thing shall be well."

The Path of the Departing Soul

BRIHADARANYAKA UPANISHAD

IV ADHYAYA, Fourth BRAHMANA

1. Yagnavalkya continued: "Now when that Self, having sunk into weakness, sinks, as it were, into unconsciousness, then gather those senses (pranas) around him, and he, taking with him those elements of light, descends into the heart. When that person in the eye turns away, then he ceases to know any forms.

2. "'He has become one,' they say, 'he does not see.' 'He has become one,' they say, 'he does not smell.' 'He has become one,' they say, 'he does not taste.' 'He has become one,' they say, 'he does not speak.' 'He has become one,' they say, 'he does not hear.' 'He has become one,' they say, 'he does not think.' 'He has become one,' they say, 'he does not touch.' 'He has become one,' they say, 'he does not know.' The point of his heart becomes lighted up, and by that light the Self departs, either through the eye, or through the skull, or through other places of the body. And when he thus departs, life (the chief prana) departs after him, and when life thus departs, all the other vital spirits (pranas) depart after it. He is conscious, and being conscious he follows and departs.

215

"Then both his knowledge and his work take hold of him, and his acquaintance with former things."

V. ADHYAYA, Tenth BRAHMANA

1. When the person goes away from this world, he comes to the wind. Then the wind makes room for him, like the hole of a carriage wheel, and through it he mounts higher. He comes to the sun. Then the sun makes room for him, like the hole of a Lambara,* and through it he mounts higher. He comes to the moon. Then the moon makes room for him, like the hole of a drum, and through it he mounts higher, and arrives at the world where there is no sorrow, no snow. There he dwells eternal years.

* *Lambara*—A musical instrument .

Acknowledgments

"The Remedies" copyright © Joseph Bruchac 1993.

"Poetry at Buchenwald" is translated by Noelle Oxenhandler from *Le Monde Commence Aujourd'hui* by Jacques Lusseyran (Paris: Le Table Ronde, 1959), pp. 115-133. Translation reprinted by permission of Noelle Oxenhandler. (To reprint, contact the translator through PARABOLA BOOKS.)

"Images of Wholeness: An Interview with Lawrence E. Sullivan" is from the "Healing" issue of PARABOLA (Vol. XVIII, No. 1), pp. 4-13.

"A Day in Court" copyright 1992: Thomas A. Dooling.

"Redeeming the Holy Sparks" © Eduardo Rauch 1993.

"The Alchemy of Illness" appeared in the "Healing" issue of PARABOLA (Vol. XVIII, No. 1), pp. 39-46. It is excerpted from the book of the same name, copyright © 1993 by Kat Duff. (New York: Pantheon, 1993). Reprinted by permission of Pantheon Books, a division of Random House, Inc.

"Flowers" is from *Partings and Other Beginnings* by Ruth Rudner (New York: The Continuum Publishing Company, 1993). Copyright © by

217

Ruth Rudner. Reprinted by permission of Ruth Rudner.

"To Reconcile Oneself With the World" by Edward Stachura, translated by Magda Zlotowska, is from the longer journal of the same title. Translation copyright © 1993 by The Continuum Publishing Group.

"The Farme of Man" by John Donne is reprinted from *Devotions*.

"Even at Night, the Sun is There" appeared in the "Healing" issue of PARABOLA (Vol. XVIII, No. 1), pp 60-65. Copyright privileges are held by the author, Gray Henry, Mockingbird Valley, Louisville, Kentucky, 40207.

"Intoxicated By My Illness" is from the book of the same title by Anatole Broyard, published by Clarkson Potter, New York, 1992, pp. 20-25, 45-46. Copyright © 1992 by Alexandra Broyard. Reprinted by permission of Clarkson N. Potter, Inc., a division of Crown Publishers, Inc.

"Germs" is from *The Lives of a Cell* by Lewis Thomas (Bantam Book, New York, 1972), pp. 88-94. "Germs" copyright © 1972 by The Massachusetts Medical Society, from *The Lives of a Cell* by Lewis Thomas. Used by permission of Viking Penguin, a division of Penquin Books USA, Inc.

"Transforming Our Suffering" appeared in the "Healing" issue of PARABOLA (Vol. XVIII, No. 1), pp. 47-49. It was adapted from *Love in Action: Writings on Nonviolent Social Change* by Thich Nhat Hanh, used with permission of Parallax Press, Berkeley, California.

"An Encounter" appeared in the "Healing" issue of PARABOLA (Vol. XVIII, No. 1), pp. 89-91. Copyright Marvin Barrett 1993.

"On Death and Coding" appeared in the "Healing" issue of PARABOLA (Vol. XVIII, No. 1), pp. 14-18. Copyright by Richard S. Sandor, M.D., 1993.

"Some Thoughts on Healing in Western Medicine" copyright Joanna M. Ward 1993.

"Word Salad" appeared in the "Healing" issue of PARABOLA (Vol. XVIII, No. 1), pp. 84-87. It is reprinted from Jay Haley, ed., *Advanced Techniques of Hypnosis and Therapy: Selected Papers of Milton Erickson, M.D.* (Needham Heights, Mass.: Allyn & Bacon, 1967), pp. 500-502. Copyright © American Journal of Clinical Hypnosis. Reprinted by permission of the American Journal of Clinical Hypnosis.

"Including Even Our Mad Parts" by Ann Belford Ulanov is excerpted from a longer article that appeared in PARABOLA under the title "The God You Touch" in the "Forgiveness" issue (Vol. XVII, No. 3), pp. 18-33. That article was adapted from a chapter in *The Christ and the Bodhisattva*, edited by Donald S. Lopez, Jr. and Steven C. Rockefeller (Albany: SUNY Press, 1987) pp. 117-139. Copyright 1987 by State University of New York Press. Reprinted by permission of Ann Belford Ulanov.

"The Healer Within" by Norman Cousins was included in *The Power to Heal: Ancient Arts & Modern Medicine* by Rick Smolan, Phillip Moffitt, and Matthew Naythons, M.D. (New York: Prentice Hall, 1990). Copyright Norman Cousins. Reprinted by permission of Eleanor Cousins.

"Spiritus Contra Spiritum" appeared in the "Addiction" issue of PARABOLA (Vol. XII, No. 2), pp. 68-71. The two letters first appeared in the January 1963 issue of The Grapevine, a monthly newsletter published by Alcoholics Anonymous. Wilson letter, copyright © The AA Grapevine, Inc., reprinted with permission. Carl Jung letter later appeared in his *Collected Letters* © 1985 by Princeton University Press. Reprinted by permission of Princeton University Press.

"A Meeting of Traditional Tibetan and Western Medicine" reprinted by permission of Keith Cohn and Lobsang Rapgay.

"Healing in Ancient Egypt" © Lise Manniche 1993.

"The Kung Approach to Healing" appeared in the "Healing" issue of PARABOLA (Vol. XVIII, No. 1), pp. 72-80 It is reprinted from Richard Katz, *Boiling Energy: Community Healing Among the Kalahari Kung* (Cambridge, Mass.: Harvard University Press, 1982). Copyright 1982 by the President and Fellows of Harvard College. Reprinted by permission of the publisher.

"The Houngan as Healer" is reprinted from Maya Deren, *Divine Horsemen: The Voodoo Gods of Haiti* (Chelsea House, New York, 1970), pp. 161-171. Reprinted by permission of the publisher.

"Navajo Sand Painting" is adapted from a longer article entitled "It's Where You Put Your Eyes" by Sam Gill in the "Storytelling and Education" issue of PARABOLA (Vol. IV, No. 4) and also included in *I Become Part of It: Sacred Dimensions in Native American Life*, edited by D.M. Dooling and Paul Jordan-Smith (PARABOLA BOOKS). Reprinted by permission of the author.

"The Powwow Doctor" appeared in the "Healing" issue of PARABOLA (Vol. XVIII, No. 1), pp. 50-55. Copyright 1993 by Richard E. Wentz. Use of material requires permission of the author.

"Mahasamadhi of Ramana Maharshi" is from Arthur Osborne's *Ramana Maharshi and the Path of Self-Knowledge* (B.I. Publications Pvt. Ltd.: New Delhi, India, 1954 and Hutchinson Books Ltd., a division of the Random Century Group, London. Reprinted by permission of the Random Century Group.

"Letting Go" appeared in the "Wholeness" issue of PARABOLA (Vol. X, No. 1), pp. 20-27. It was subsequently included in *Leaning on the Moment*, a selection of interviews from PARABOLA, published by PARABOLA BOOKS. Reprinted by permission of Helen M. Luke.

"The Path of the Departing Soul" is from the Brihadaranyaka Upanishad, translated by F. Max Muller in *The Sacred Books of the East*, Vol. XV, reprinted by Dover Publications, New York, from the original edition published by the Clarendon Press, Oxford, 1884.

Contributors

Marvin Barrett is the author of *Spare Days* and the forthcoming *The Consolations of Age*. He is a senior editor of PARABOLA.

Anatole Broyard, longtime book reviewer for *The New York Times*, chronicled his own terminal illness with cancer in *Intoxicated By My Illness* (Clarkson Potter). His memoir of his life as a writer in New York's Greenwich Village literary community, *Kafka Was the Rage*, was released by Carol Southern Books in late 1993. He died in 1990.

Joseph Bruchac is an Abenaki storyteller and writer. He is the editor of The Greenfield Review and a contributing editor of PARABOLA.

Keith Cohn is a San Francisco cardiologist and director of cardiology education at the California Pacific Medical Center. He is co-author, with Darby Duke, of *Coming Back* (Addison-Wesley), a book on heart-attacks.

Norman Cousins (1915-1990) was the editor of Saturday Review from 1940-1971 and was the author of *Anatomy of an Illness* and *The Healing Heart*.

Maya Deren (1908-1961) was an experimental filmmaker who spent many years in Haiti. Her unfinished film and her book, *Divine*

Horsemen: The Voodoo Gods of Haiti, both chronicle the island and its religious and ritual customs.

John Donne (1573-1631) was an English metaphysical poet and preacher. Born a Catholic, he converted to the Anglican church in 1615 and was dean of St. Paul's Cathedral in London, where he frequently preached before Charles I.

Thomas A. Dooling is a writer, lawyer, and cashmere goat breeder in Dillon, Montana. He has contributed a number of articles to PARABOLA.

Kat Duff is a counselor in private practice in northern New Mexico. She won the 1991 Taos Review literary contest for non-fiction.

Milton Erickson (1901-1980), a leading medical practitioner of hypnosis in the twentieth century, was the founding president of the American Society for Clinical Hypnosis.

Sam Gill is professor of religion at the University of Colorado in Boulder. He is the author of several books on Navajo religion and *Mother Earth: The American Story.* (University of Chicago Press).

Thich Nhat Hanh is a Vietnamese Zen master and poet. He headed the Buddhist delegation during the Paris Peace Accords in 1969. His books include *Being Peace* (Parallax Press, 1987) and *The Miracle of Mindfulness* (Beacon Press, 1988).

Gray Henry is director of the American Branch of Quinta Essentia and of the Islamic Texts Society.

Hippocrates (460-377 BC) was a Greek physician who is considered the father of modern medicine, although some scholars have questioned that he actually authored The Hippocratic Oath, a pledge still found on many physicians' walls.

Carl G. Jung (1875-1961) was the founder of a leading school of modern psychotherapy, incorporating mythology and archetypal symbols into the study of human psychology. He is the author of *Man and His Symbols* and *Memories, Dreams, Reflections*, as well as numerous other studies.

Richard Katz is a professor at the Saskatchewan Indian Federated College, Saskatoon, Saskatchewan, Canada. His books include *Nobody's Child* and *The Straight Path* (Addison-Wesley).

Helen M. Luke is a Jungian counselor and the founder of the Apple Farm Community near Three Rivers, Michigan. She is the author of *Dark Wood to White Rose*, a study of Dante's *Divine Comedy*, and two collections of essays, *Old Age* and *Kaleidoscope* (all PARABOLA BOOKS).

Jacques Lusseyran (1924-1971) is the author of *And There Was Light* (PARABOLA BOOKS), an account of his founding of a resistance group of young people in Paris during World War II. Blind from the age of 8, Lusseyran was eventually captured by the Germans and survived imprisonment at Buchenwald concentration camp.

Lise Manniche is the author of several works on ancient Egypt, including *An Ancient Egyptian Herbal* (Kegan Paul International) and *Music and Musicians in Ancient Egypt* (British Museum Press).

Arthur Osborne was an English student of Hinduism and Vedanta who became a disciple of Ramana Maharshi. He edited the complete works of Ramana Maharshi and wrote other books on Maharshi and his teachings, as well as a life of Sai Baba. He lived for 20 years in Maharshi's ashram and edited the journal The Mountain Path there. He died in 1971.

Lobsang Rapgay has a doctorate in Buddhist healing and psychology from Visva Bharati University in India. He was director of the Tibetan Holistic Medical Center in New Delhi and is former deputy secretary at the office of His Holiness the Dalai Lama. He is presently doing post-doctoral research in psychology at UCLA.

Eduardo Rauch, a native of Chile, is co-director of the Melton Research Center of the Jewish Theological Seminary in New York and recently edited two issues of The Melton Journal there on the connections between ecology and the Jewish tradition.

Ruth Rudner makes her home in Montana and is the author of *Bitterroot to Beartooth: Hiking Southwest Montana* (Sierra Club Books) and *Partings and Other Beginnings* (Continuum).

223

Richard S. Sandor lives in Los Angeles. He is a doctor of psychiatry, specializing in addiction treatment, and a member of the clinical faculty at the UCLA School of Medicine.

Edward Stachura (1937-1979) was a Polish poet, novelist and songwriter who chronicled his own disability and suicide in his last published work, *To Reconcile Oneself with the World*.

Lawrence E. Sullivan is the Director of the Center for the Study of World Religions at Harvard University. He is the author of *Icanchu's Drum* and the editor of *Healing and Restoring: Health and Medicine in the World's Religious Traditions* (both Macmillan).

Lewis Thomas is a physician and writer. His books include *Lives of a Cell* and *Medusa and the Snail*.

Ann Belford Ulanov is professor of psychiatry and religion at Union Theological Seminary in New York City. With her husband Barry, she is author of *The Witch and the Clown: Two Archetypes of Human Sexuality* (Chiron Books).

Joanna M. Ward lives in London. She is a retired dermatologist with an interest in alternative medicine.

Richard Wentz, a native of Pennsylvania, is professor of religious studies at Arizona State University. His books include *Pennsylvania Dutch Folk Spirituality* (Paulist Press) and *Religion in the New World: The Shaping of Religious Traditions in the United States* (Fortress Press).

Bill Wilson (1895-1971) was the co-founder, with Dr. Robert Smith, of Alcoholics Anonymous in 1935.

Index